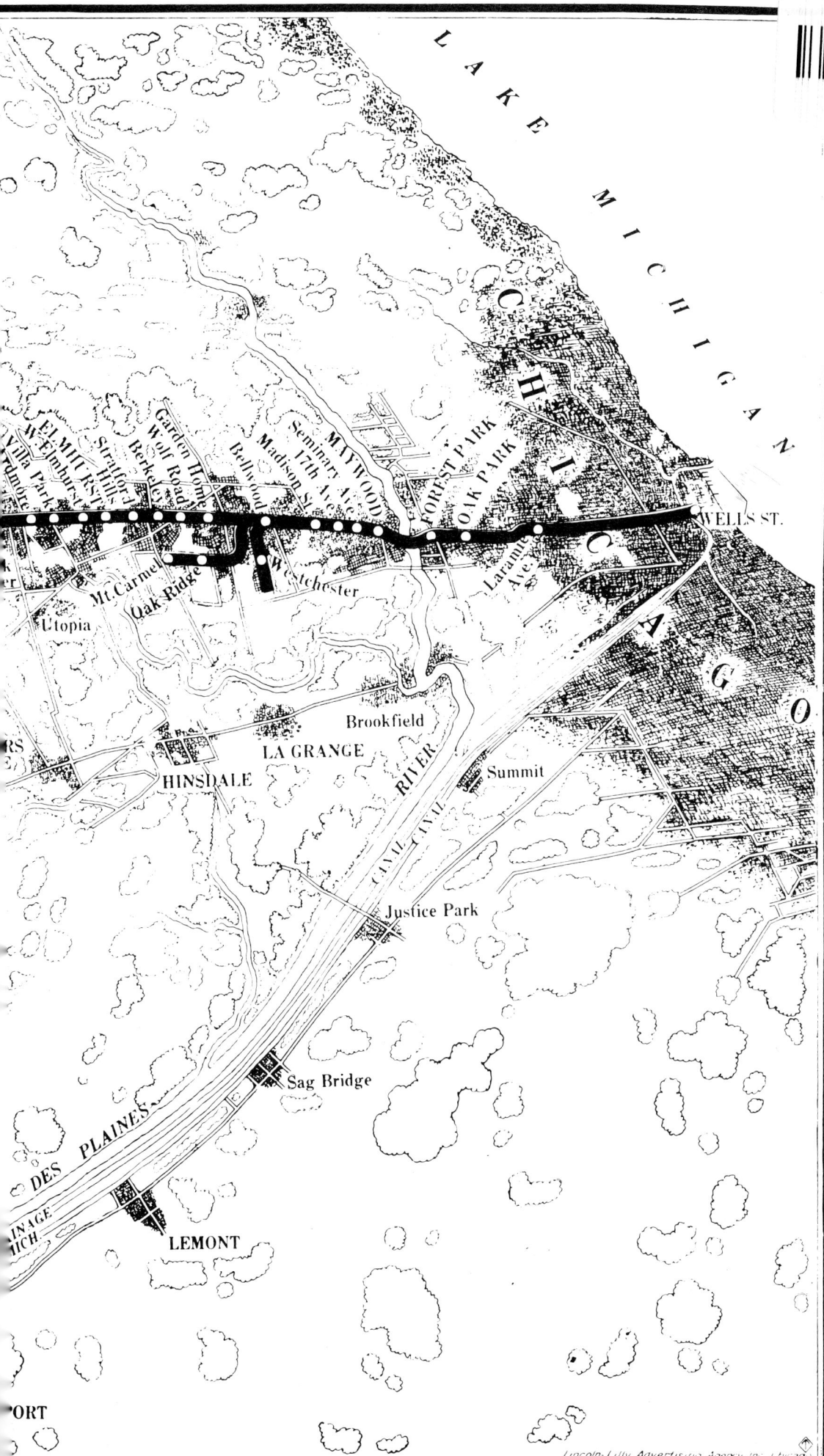

This map appeared in a booklet issued by the Chicago Aurora & Elgin Railroad in 1926. It shows all trackage owned or operated by the CA&E with the exception of the short segment from Geneva to St. Charles which was operated over the tracks of the Aurora Elgin & Fox River Electric line.

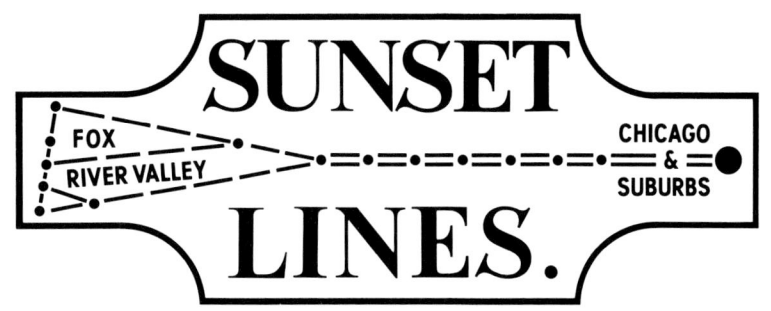

The Story of the Chicago Aurora & Elgin Railroad

1 — Trackage

Larry Plachno

GORDON E. LLOYD / LARRY PLACHNO COLLECTION.

SUNSET LINES.

The Story of The Chicago Aurora & Elgin Railroad
1 — Trackage

by Larry Plachno

DOUG CHRISTIANSEN / GREG HEIER COLLECTION

The Chicago Aurora & Elgin is unique among electric interurban railways. It was the first true high-speed interurban to be built, and it started service with the most powerful cars then in existence. For over five decades it scheduled mile-a-minute trains over most of its trackage. It originally operated in typical interurban fashion with milk trains, newspaper trains, and an occasional parlor car. But, in later years, it became more of a commuter line connecting Chicago's Loop with affluent Du Page County suburbs while trying to gain a foothold in the carload freight business. The nickname "Sunset Lines" was adopted at an early date since evening trains left Chicago and headed west, to the Fox River Valley and into the sunset.

Interest in the railroad has remained high since the Chicago Aurora & Elgin was one of the last interurbans to face economic reality and abandon operations. It was also one of the few railroads to discontinue passenger service in the middle of the day while still operating a relatively complete schedule.

Volume 1 provides a detailed review of the company's routes and trackage with track maps, text and photos. Two additional volumes are planned covering the history, operations and equipment of the Chicago Aurora & Elgin.

DANIEL E. FRIZANE

Sunset Lines
The Story of the
Chicago Aurora & Elgin Railroad
1 — Trackage

by Larry Plachno

Copyright © 1986 by Transportation Trails

All Rights Reserved

No part of this book may be reproduced in any manner whatsoever without written permission from the publisher, except in the case of brief quotations embodied in reviews and articles.

Transportation Trails
9698 West Judson Road
Polo, Illinois 61064
Phone: (815) 946-2341

First Printing: December 1986
Manufactured in the United States of America

Information on similar books or following books in this series is available on written or phone request.

Library of Congress Cataloging in Publication Data

Plachno, Larry, 1943-
   Sunset Lines.

   Bibliography: V. 3, p.
   Includes Indexes.
   Contents: v. 1. Trackage.
   1. Chicago, Aurora & Elgin Railroad. 2. Street-railroads—Illinois—Chicago Metropolitan Area.
I. Title
TF725.C42P56   1986   385'.5   86-30751
ISBN 0-933449-02-X (v. 1)

Publisher's Credits

electronic typesetting and page layout: Larry Plachno, National Bus Trader, Inc., Polo, Illinois.
chapter heading / cover art: Chuck Boie, The Art Factory, Ltd., Elm Grove, Wisconsin.
track maps: Roy G. Benedict, Chicago, Illinois.
printing: Rochelle Printing Co., Rochelle, Illinois.
binding: Zonne Book Binders, Chicago, Illinois.

Table of Contents

	Dedication	7
	Introduction	9
	Preface	11
	Acknowledgements	13
1	The Super Interurban *(Setting the record straight)*	15
2	Chicago's Insull Interurbans *(Comparing the big three)*	19
3	Wells Street Terminal *(The terminal at Chicago's loop)*	27
4	On The "L" *(Shared trackage with the "L" from Wells Street to Forest Park)*	33
5	Forest Park *(The eastern terminal in the last years)*	45
6	Double Track Through Suburbia *(The double track speedway from Forest Park to Wheaton)*	51
7	Westchester and Mt. Carmel/Cook County Branches *(The two short branches south of the main line)*	71
8	Wheaton *(Major junction, shops and yard for the CA&E)*	81
9	Aurora Branch *(The branch from Wheaton to Aurora)*	91
10	Batavia Branch *(From Eola Junction to Batavia)*	109
11	Elgin Branch *(The branch from Wheaton to Elgin)*	119
12	Geneva Branch *(From Geneva Junction to Geneva and St. Charles)*	137
13	Photographs *(Color and black & white photos of the CA&E along the line)*	145
	Index	158

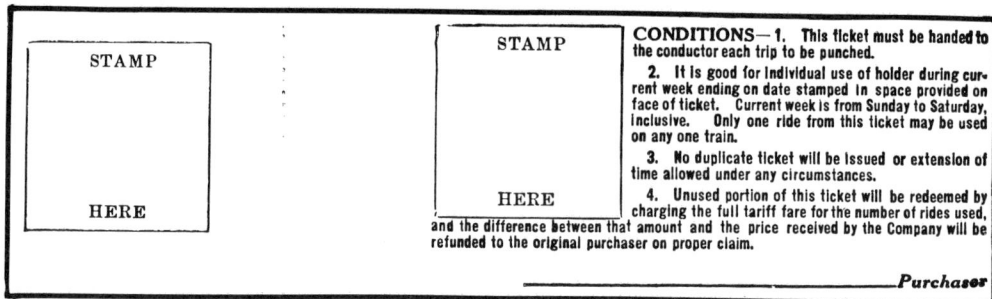

Top: Chicago Aurora & Elgin cash fare receipt issued by the crew for fares paid on the train.

Above: Front and back of a one-week, 12-ride commutation ticket. The tear-off stub was the first ride, the next ten rides were punched, and the last ride was the remaining coupon.

Left and Below: Front and back of four employee pass coupons.

Dedication

Family tradition holds that I started chasing trains before I could walk. My father was always a railroad commuter and the family home at the time of my birth was adjacent to the Milwaukee Road on Chicago's north side. It was reported that I expressed an abnormal interest in those big steam locomotives on the Milwaukee Road tracks.

By the time I started school, my family had moved to Bensenville, Illinois. If a ride was not available, the walk to school consumed about a mile down what was then farm roads and across the Milwaukee Road tracks. Watching those locomotives and trains was a delight, particularly the evening fast freight which warranted a locomotive obviously larger than the commuter trains. In later years a park was built along my old school route and a small steam locomotive appropriately enshrined along the Milwaukee Road tracks.

At some point during 1950 I was bundled into the family car and participated in a ride to the DuPage County seat at Wheaton, probably to renew Dad's driver's license. During that trip I "discovered" the Chicago Aurora & Elgin in Wheaton and soon became totally interested in a railroad with big red and blue cars which did not use steam locomotives. I soon requested that my seventh birthday be celebrated with a ride on the Chicago Aurora & Elgin. And since Dad was somewhat interested in railroads and traction himself, it did not take much persuasion to get my request accepted.

So on a remarkably pleasant day in late 1950, this man and his son appeared at the Wells Street Terminal in Chicago. I was fortunate in being able to watch a train being made up and was particularly curious about the MU jumper cables being used to connect the cars.

For some unknown reason, I selected Elgin as a destination which meant that I would not be in the lead car for some of the trip. However, I did ride in the front "railfan" seat and was particularly pleased when we headed up the Elgin branch and I could watch the motorman. Time permitted a brief walk in Elgin and then the ride back to Chicago. Because of the winter season it was dark by the time we got back to Chicago, but I kept my nose to that front window until we returned to Wells Street.

Soon thereafter I also "discovered" the North Shore Line and was treated to my first Electroliner trip by Dad. As I became a teenager, I frequently was able to spend a delightful day on my own riding the North Shore Line or South Shore Line, but the CA&E always remained my favorite and I made several trips to Wheaton after passenger service had been discontinued.

Dad has since retired to California but continues to read all the traction material I send him. He is now looking forward to a return of the trolley cars in San Jose.

Hence, I would like to dedicate this book to my father, Joseph John Plachno, who introduced me to the Chicago Aurora & Elgin. Were it not for his interest in the CA&E, and transportation in general, this book would most likely never have been written.

Larry Plachno
Polo, Illinois
September 19, 1986

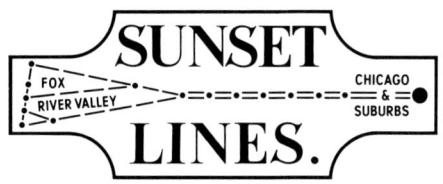

The illustration at the top depicts the logo of the Aurora Elgin & Chicago Railway Co., predecessor to the Chicago Aurora & Elgin.

The Sunset Lines name was never officially adopted by the CA&E, but this logo appeared on the sides of cars for many years.

The official logo of the Chicago Aurora & Elgin was created during the 1920's and survived in use until the end of operations.

Introduction

Transportation in America has undergone a remarkable change in the past century and a half. As recently as the early 1800's, any serious long distance travel was accomplished by boat or ship on the ocean, rivers, or canals. Local travel was slow and tedious, accomplished by horse and wagon on muddy and usually non-existant roads.

The first railway in the United States was established in 1831, and soon changed the basic transportation picture. It was now possible for passengers and merchandise to travel overland with some degree of speed and safety.

Railway technology was soon applied to solve the need for local transportation within growing cities. At first, horses and mules were used to pull little passenger cars along primitive railroad tracks set in local streets. By 1890, the technology of electricity had advanced to a point where it became a suitable source of power for street railways. Within a very short time, electric trolley cars began replacing the horsecars used for local transportation within cities. Before long, the promoters of the electric street railways began to look beyond the city limits and to project electric railways into the surrounding rural areas and to neighboring communities. These longer-distance lines soon became known as electric interurban railways.

The first decade of this century witnessed a major investment and building boom in interurban electric railways. Strangely enough, it was during this same period that Henry Ford found difficulty in obtaining financing to produce automobiles. But the interurban railways were originally seen as a modern and practical means of transportation.

The interurbans provided fast, frequent and economical transportation between neighboring cities. They also provided transportation for rural residents and farmers. In most areas, the building of a new interurban into a community was cause for great celebration. Although most major communities were served by steam railroads, the interurbans were a boon to rural residents and farmers since they provided frequent and inexpensive service to smaller towns and to virtually any crossroad on the line. For the first time, it became possible for shoppers to go into the big city and return in a day, for salesmen to make several local calls in one day, and for milk and packages to be shipped to and from rural locations quickly and with ease. The interurbans provided the first meaningful transportation for large sections of rural America.

By 1910, interurban lines served most major communities in Ohio, Indiana, Illinois, Pennsylvania and Southern Michigan. Similar lines were built in other states but were less popular.

The early electric interurban railways used passenger cars not much different from the early city streetcars. As time went on, most interurban railways began using passenger cars which were closer to steam railroad equipment but still very similar to city streetcars in their use of electricity for power. In fact, most interurban railways used city streetcar tracks as a means to enter or pass through cities. Some interurban lines generated sufficient long-distance ridership to warrant investing in parlor cars, dining cars, or even sleeping cars. However, the typical interurban railway was a local entity serving local needs. It was only in rare situations that interurban railways were able to compete with the steam railroads in the area of long distance travel.

This dependance upon local patronage proved to be a financial disaster to the interurban industry. The development of the automobile and paved roads drew away most interurban passengers and decimated the industry. By 1932, half of all interurban lines had ceased operations or at least had given up passenger service. By the late 1940's, only a handful of interurban lines remained, usually those that had developed substantial freight or commuter traffic. None survived as typical, rural interurban lines, although some former interurban trackage remains in use today for freight or commuter service.

The Chicago Aurora & Elgin Railroad was a small but significant part of the interurban industry. In many respects, it was typical of the industry in that it was founded to connect rural areas and smaller communities to the nearby city. Like most interurbans, it had a policy of providing fast, frequent service. In other respects, the Chicago Aurora & Elgin was substantially different than most interurbans. Initial construction and speeds were considerably above normal for an interurban. As the rural areas began developing into suburbs, the Chicago Aurora & Elgin became a major commuter carrier and continued operations well beyond the time when most other interurban lines had thrown in the towel and ripped up their tracks. The Chicago Aurora & Elgin was, at least initially, innovative and progressive. When designed and built, it was clearly a step above and beyond other interurban lines of the same era — truly the first high-speed, high-quality interurban. In later years, a few other interurban lines were able to match this speed and quality, but the Chicago Aurora & Elgin outlived almost all of them and became one of the better known interurbans.

The story of the Chicago Aurora & Elgin is one of transition. When initially built as the Aurora Elgin & Chicago, the railroad was similar to other interurbans in that it served rural communities, cut across farmland, and even operated special milk trains. After 50 years of suburban growth, the Chicago Aurora & Elgin had evolved into what was primarily an electric commuter line. Likewise, the Aurora Elgin & Chicago in 1902 was considered the most modern and highest development of a high speed interurban railroad. A half-century later, the early achievements were forgotten and the CA&E had become somewhat of an anachronism.

Above all else, and in spite of its occasional shortcomings, the Chicago Aurora & Elgin was beloved by its passengers and commuters. The morning commuters would gather at suburban stations at train time to board their regular trains toward the rising sun. The convenient one-seat ride to Chicago's Loop, the friendly train crews, the comfortable old cars, and the traditional banter between the regular commuters gave the impression of a private club. Evening saw the reverse procedure as commuters rode home toward the sunset. This same scene was repeated every weekday for decades until passenger service was abruptly discontinued on July 3, 1957. The commuters found alternate means of transportation but most agreed that commuting was not as convenient nor as pleasant after the demise of the CA&E.

Train operations towards the setting sun were noted and the name "Sunet Lines" was adopted by the interurban at an early date. Although never used as an official title, the "Sunset Lines" name and design did appear on the cars and on printed material for many years. Initially, it had been our intention to title these volumes "The Super Interurban" because of the extraordinary aspects of the Aurora Elgin & Chicago at the time of its construction. However, the somewhat unofficial but appropriate nickname "Sunset Lines" was eventually selected as the title for these volumes on the Chicago Aurora & Elgin since it was used extensively throughout most of the life of the interurban and was popular with the commuters and friends of the line.

Chicago Aurora & Elgin St. Louis car #455 rests at the Wheaton yard between assignments in June of 1946. The St. Louis cars were brand new at this time and were the last new passenger coaches purchased by the CA&E. TIMOTHY C. IVERSON COLLECTION.

Preface

1984 marked a quarter of a century since the power was turned off for the last time on the Chicago Aurora & Elgin. This 25th anniversary of final electric operation brought some special attention to the memory of the 'Roarin' Elgin, particularly at the operating museums. At that time, it was noted that there had only been two books published on the Chicago Aurora & Elgin, with the most recent already being 19 years old.

By late 1984, we had decided that it was time for another book on the Chicago Aurora & Elgin, and we decided to tackle such a project during 1985. Admittedly, our original intention involved nothing more than a small photo album on this third rail interurban. As a result, a request went out in early 1985 seeking the use of photos for such a book. Several traction hobbyists opened their photo collections to us, and the project was soon underway.

At the same time, we were contacted by several individuals who felt that our effort could well end up being the last volume published on the Chicago Aurora & Elgin. As a result, they opened their historical collections to us and encouraged us to expand the scope of our book from a mere photo album to something more closely approaching a definitive history. Since the 'Roarin' Elgin had always been my favorite interurban, I quickly agreed. At that time I did not fully appreciate what these people had in mind and were willing to support.

Adding this additional historical material to our text proved easier than one might imagine. This book was entered on our new typesetting system which combines the attributes of a computer, word processor, and typesetter into a single system. Consequently, it was relatively easy to insert material in a specified location, move entire paragraphs and sections to a different part of the book, and create new chapters at will.

At one point our office began to look like a traction archive as several cartons of photographic and historical data on the Chicago Aurora & Elgin were carefully examined and then entered into the ever-growing data base. On at least two occasions, substantial piles of additional data were received and the process began all over again. The original chapters were expanded, subdivided, and expanded again. By late 1985, it became obvious that the text had not only grown well beyond our original plans, but had also exceeded the appropriate size for a single volume. Hence, we decided to split the final data into at least three volumes for publication.

At one point, we had plans to enter all of the material into our computer typesetting system prior to publishing the first volume. This idea was given up in early 1986 when we realized that there was still a substantial amount of work to be done to complete the total text, but that almost all of this work was in the areas of history and equipment. Hence, we decided to move ahead with publishing the first volume even though we still had portions to complete on the second and third volumes.

This first volume covers the trackage of the Chicago Aurora & Elgin with primary emphasis on the later years of operation. Trackage was selected as the topic for this first volume because it was the one area of the text closest to completion. In addition, we felt that the track maps would assist the reader in better understanding the material to follow in later volumes. To a large extent, the material in this first volume is better known than the material to follow in subsequent volumes. However, we felt that a review of trackage was a necessary starting point for an interurban history of this magnitude.

As indicated, this first volume covers Chicago Aurora & Elgin trackage during the later years of operation. We have subdivided the CA&E into several logical sections and have provided a track map, text, and photos for each section. This is not intended to be a photo album. Instead, the photographs generally follow a geographical sequence in each chapter. They cover all major (and many minor) points of interest along the CA&E, with very little duplication of scene. We apologize in advance for some photos of lesser quality, but we felt that they were necessary to make the coverage as complete as possible.

We expect that at least two additional volumes will be produced in this series to complete this story of the Chicago Aurora & Elgin. This additional material will include a substantial chronological history of the interurban from the early planning days through final scrapping operations. Other areas of coverage include freight operations, funeral car service, the Cannonball, bus service, other special operations, and a review of equipment. Most of this text has already been completed and publication of these two volumes should follow as time permits.

In scope, these three volumes will cover the trackage, history, and operations of the Chicago Aurora & Elgin. The Fox River lines and other connecting lines are mentioned only when they impact the CA&E.

Since these initial three volumes will be considered a set, we have elected to hold off publishing the bibliography until the third volume. Hence, it will cover the research material used in all three volumes. We will, however, include an index for each volume.

We do wish to leave the door open for the possibility of additional volumes beyond number three. The Fox River Trolley Lines, additional history, and oral history have already been suggested as appropriate topics for possible volumes to follow.

In spite of all of our efforts, there still are certain aspects of CA&E history which are unclear at this point. For example, we have not yet been able to develop a CA&E bus roster, and the situations surrounding the founding of the Chicago Wheaton & Western as well as the 1953 cutback in service are still unclear. In addition, we are still seeking the use of photographs and slides for future volumes, particularly those of the early days or including the parlor cars, funeral trains, milk service, etc. Any assistance in this regard would be greatly appreciated.

Articles and information on the Chicago Aurora & Elgin appear regularly in FIRST AND FASTEST, the magazine of the Shore Line Interurban Historical Society. Any clarifications and additions, as well as information on these volumes, will also be mentioned in FIRST AND FASTEST. Membership information can be obtained by writing: Shore Line Interurban Historical Society, Post Office Box 346, Chicago, Illinois 60690.

At its founding, the Chicago Aurora & Elgin represented a substantial technological advancement over its contemporaries. In similar fashion, the production of this book represents a similar advancement. As early as April of 1985, we began setting type using a diskette-based, computer-controlled typesetting system. Due to state-of-the art technology, we are now able to produce total pages intact from the typesetting system and eliminate any need for paste-up other than artwork. With the exception of the drawing for chapter headings, all of the text pages in this book were produced intact from our typesetting system and required no paste-up.

Larry Plachno
Polo, Illinois
September 18, 1986

Chicago Aurora & Elgin Cincinnati car #423 poses at the north side of the yard in Wheaton. In the background is the embankment for the branch to Elgin. DANIEL E. FRIZANE COLLECTION.

Acknowledgements

Your author is quick to acknowledge that no project of this magnitude can be credited to a single individual. The comprehensiveness of the material, historical coverage, and photography in this and following volumes in this series on the Chicago Aurora & Elgin should be credited to several individuals. These historians, traction fans and photographers joined in by generously and unselfishly lending their photographs, historical material and time to this effort.

This project initially got underway when several individuals lent us their Chicago Aurora & Elgin photo collections for use in these books. Included in this initial group were Gordon E. Lloyd, Terry L. McConnell, Dan Frizane, William E. Robertson, William C. Hoffman and Malcolm D. McCarter. Larry Kostka also provided some supurb color slides. At a later date, other photos were submitted by Timothy C. Iverson, Victor G. Wagner and George Krambles. A special acknowledgement must be made to Richard G. Allermann, who has a massive collection of several hundred CA&E photos and slides, and who made his entire collection available to us. Without his assistance this first volume would have been impossible to illustrate. In addition, we acknowledge the contributions of other photographers, some unknown, whose excellent photographs of the Chicago Aurora & Elgin reached us through secondary sources and current owners.

To Steve Hyett goes credit for encouraging us to initially expand the historical sections of our project. He also provided a great deal of historical information and several photographs. Greg Heier warrants special mention. He made several trips to our office to present us with hundreds of photos and slides to be used on this project. He also provided a substantial amount of historical information gleaned from the old Wheaton newspapers.

A special thanks goes to John D. Horachek, a North Shore Line historian who provided his extensive CA&E historical file gleaned from old trade magazines which proved invaluable for the second volume in this series. Eric Bronsky of the Shore Line Interurban Historical Society deserves special mention for his words of encouragement, historical material, and for locating several excellent photographs.

Thanks to Bill Nedden who assisted with some of the earlier organization of this material. Thanks to Paul Leger, Melvin Bernero and Bruce Moffat who graciously assisted in historical information and photos of the CA&E bus operations for that section in a future volume. Thanks also to Steve Michaels for spending several evenings going through the old CA&E corporate ledgers to glean interesting information.

Proofing of some of the early material was accomplished by Greg Heier, Jim Johnson, Gordon E. Lloyd, Steve Hyett, Eric Bronsky and Bob Gibson. Both Greg Heier and Eric Bronsky gave substantially of their time to assist in the final proofing of this volume. Credit for the excellent track maps in this first volume goes to Roy G. Benedict. And Chuck Boie deserves credit for the fine artwork used on the cover and as a chapter heading.

Thanks also to anyone who may have assisted in some way but whose name may not have been known to us or who may have been inadvertently overlooked.

Last, but not least, a special thanks to my wife, Jackie, for encouragement and untold hours of proofreading — even though her only ride on a CA&E car came after abandonment at railroad museums.

Larry Plachno
September 16, 1986

1

The Super Interurban

Those individuals who take a special interest in the Chicago Aurora & Elgin may be delighted to hear that it deserves a loftier position in interurban history than it has previously been given. Earlier histories have treated the Chicago Aurora & Elgin as just another interurban line. However, extensive research into the Chicago Aurora & Elgin and its predecessors has shown that it was very special and deserves to be remembered for both its contributions and unique standing in interurban history.

The reasons are obvious as to why the Chicago Aurora & Elgin has not received the credit to which it was due. When examined from the standpoint of the 1960's, the CA&E was hampered by its proximity to the successful North Shore Line and South Shore Line. Although surviving most other interurbans, the CA&E failed to outlive its two neighboring lines in Chicago. And, by the 1960's, the major contributions of the CA&E had substantially been forgotten. Hence, it was relegated to a somewhat secondary position in history.

However, a step back several decades reveals an entirely different situation. When the Aurora Elgin & Chicago (predecessor to the CA&E) first started operations, STREET RAILWAY JOURNAL stated: "It is seldom that the inauguration of any single electric railway enterprise makes such an important advance in the art as has that of the Aurora Elgin & Chicago Railway."

When built, the Aurora Elgin & Chicago was a revolutionary super interurban with better trackage, more powerful cars and faster speeds than any previous (and most later) interurbans. It was the talk of the industry and the mark by which other interurbans were measured. The AE&C also revolutionized many aspects of interurban planning and construction.

It is interesting to note that in late 1902, the Aurora Elgin & Chicago was dispatching regular runs that knocked off mile-a-minute speeds while the predecessor to the North Shore Line was still a country trolley line. Some later interurbans attempted to imitate the Aurora Elgin & Chicago, but few ever came close.

To the discredit of the AE&C, and later the CA&E, it was unable to expand upon its early advantage and essentially spent a half-century resting on its early triumphs. Nonetheless, the Chicago Aurora & Elgin did rack up several impressive attributes and unique features. Among these are the following:

• The Aurora Elgin & Chicago was built as the nation's first high-speed interurban line. In spite of being somewhat unique and experimental, it was also highly successful and served as a model for many of the more successful interurban lines which were built in later years. It probably can be said that the opening of the AE&C was the single most progressive and innovative interurban railway opening in the history of the industry.

• The first order of passenger cars for the AE&C were the most powerful and probably the fastest interurban cars in existence at that time.

• When constructed, the Aurora Elgin & Chicago had a right-of-way equal to general steam railroad standards except for street operations in Aurora (which were eliminated decades later). Very few other interurban lines ever came close to matching the AE&C in this regard.

• In spite of the fact that its planning and development took place in the earliest and pioneering years of the interurban era, the AE&C managed to select what eventually became the most popular and practical power distribution system among interurbans. This included high voltage alternating current from the powerhouse to the substations, and low voltage direct current power to the cars. During this same era, such well-known companies as the Illinois Traction, Chicago Lake Shore & South Bend, and the Milwaukee Electric were experimenting with alternating current power to their cars. Virtually all interurbans eventually used a similar system to that initially installed on the AE&C in 1902.

• The Chicago Aurora & Elgin was so highly regarded that it was at one time or another controlled by four well-known interurban syndicates or management groups. Most interurban lines did well to attract one.

PRECEDING PAGE

Car #318 pauses on the Clintonville siding while operating a special trip for railfans. #318 was the only one of six Jewett cars built in 1913 with steel sheathing on the sides. GREG HEIER COLLECTION.

Sunset Lines • 15

Above: The CA&E operated both the first and last high speed U.S.-built interurban cars. St. Louis car #453 heads the first excursion with the new cars near Prince Crossing on a very cold winter day in late 1945. GREG HEIER COLLECTION.

Below: CA&E #7 rests in front of the Wheaton shops in a photo taken during the 1950's. Originally built as an express car, #7 was later turned into a tool car. LARRY PLACHNO COLLECTION.

- Unlike most interurban lines and railroads, the Chicago Aurora & Elgin enjoyed an almost continual increase in patronage from its first day of operation until almost the end. The two major exceptions were the late teen years and the Depression. The high point of passenger revenue came in 1947, only ten years prior to the discontinuance of passenger service.
- An extremely rare attribute of the Chicago Aurora & Elgin was that it never retired a series of cars by replacement with new equipment. Individual cars were occasionally retired due to accidents or conversion to special purpose equipment, but new cars were always an addition to the fleet and not a replacement.
- The Chicago Aurora & Elgin was almost always short of equipment. The Aurora Elgin & Chicago started operations in 1902 with an absolute minimum of equipment. With only minor exceptions, this situation persisted until 1953 when service was cut back to Forest Park.
- The Chicago Aurora & Elgin (and predecessor) ordered and operated the first and the last high speed U.S.-built interurban cars.
- The Aurora Elgin & Chicago and the Chicago Aurora & Elgin operated high speed interurban service over virtually its entire line from 1902 to 1957 — a total of 55 years. With the possible exception of the South Shore Line, no other interurban attained a similar record.
- During its last decade of passenger service, the CA&E operated a fleet that spanned a distance of 45 years in construction dates, yet was relatively similar. It is doubtful that any other interurban could make a similar claim.
- The Chicago Aurora & Elgin was the last interurban to purchase wooden cars for commercial passenger service.
- Unlike virtually all other interurban lines and railroads, the Chicago Aurora & Elgin never operated a fleet of combination baggage and passenger cars (combines). There was only one car in the fleet that could be classed as a combine (old #10), and it was used in funeral car service at times.
- All of the interurban passenger cars owned by the Chicago Aurora & Elgin, and the third rail division of the Aurora Elgin & Chicago, (which excludes suburban car #500) were capable of operating over the west side elevated tracks.

Most of these attributes and features will be discussed in volumes two and three of this series.

On rare occasions, Chicago Aurora & Elgin cars left their home rails for special duties elsewhere. Such was the case during World War II when increased activity at the Great Lakes Naval Training Station promted the North Shore Line to borrow CA&E cars. On July 4, 1942, CA&E Cincinnati car #422 brought up the rear of a special sailor train pulling into the Milwaukee Terminal of the North Shore Line. DOUGLAS TRAXLER.

2

Chicago's Insull Interurbans

The Chicago Aurora & Elgin is best known and best remembered as one of the three "Chicago Insull Interurban" electric railroads. The other two members of this trio included the Chicago North Shore & Milwaukee and the Chicago South Shore & South Bend. Of the three, time has forced the Chicago Aurora & Elgin into a position of being the least known, the least remembered, and the least published of the three. This turn of events is very unfortunate since the CA&E had a unique personality all its own and in some respects was actually superior to the other two members of this trio.

In addition to the obvious similarity of interurban electric operation, the CA&E claimed several aspects in common with the North Shore Line and the South Shore Line. All three came under the control of Insull interests and were improved and modernized at that time. The CA&E received the least benefit from Insull control since it had initially been built to extremely high standards and had also been improved considerably under the Conway reorganization. All three companies engaged in bus operations at one time or another, usually starting in the 1920's. The CA&E had the smallest bus operation of the three, yet was the only one to retain bus operation until the end of passenger service.

All three companies differed from the typical interurban in having double-ended cars and in developing substantial commuter patronage. While most interurbans operated single ended cars, the CA&E, North Shore Line and South Shore Line all operated double ended cars with train doors. This was undoubtedly a reflection on a need to run multiple car trains due to substantial patronage. In addition, the three companies did not have loops at terminal points to turn single ended equipment. All three companies also enjoyed a longevity well beyond virtually all passenger carrying interurban lines.

THE CA&E AS A LEADER

From a positive standpoint, the Chicago Aurora & Elgin could claim some areas of superiority over its neighboring interurban electric railroads. In 1905, the CA&E obtained trackage rights over the elevated line into Chicago, thus making it the first interurban railroad to reach a downtown terminal over rapid transit trackage. This also made the CA&E the first electric railroad (other than the local streetcars, rapid transit lines and the Tunnel Company) to reach downtown Chicago. In comparison, the Chicago South Shore & South Bend did not operate its cars into downtown Chicago under electric power until 1926.

At least initially, the CA&E was also superior from the standpoint of right-of-way and operations. Due mainly to the backing of Cleveland financial syndicates, the CA&E started operations in 1902 as a high-speed railroad. In fact, in 1902 the line was considered a "super interurban" and vastly superior to other lines then in operation. By comparison, the North Shore Line started out as a local trolley line and did not really attain high-speed operation until the line from Waukegan to Milwaukee was built. Actual completion of a high-speed right-of-way over most of the route did not come until 1926 when Insull management built the Skokie Valley Line. The South Shore Line had the advantage of starting with a relatively good right-of-way but was hindered by the lack of a Chicago entrance and good equipment. Both were resolved by the Insull management in the 1920's.

The CA&E was also the only one of the three major Chicago interurbans that could boast involvement by four major electric railway groups or syndicates at one time or another. The line was originally founded by groups affiliated with both the famed Everett-Moore syndicate and the Pomeroy-Mandelbaum syndicate. These are generally considered to be the two largest interurban railway construction and operation syndicates at the turn of the century. In the 1920's, the CA&E was rescued from receivership by a group head-

---

PRECEDING PAGE

Although the CA&E ordered the last conventional cars built for a U.S. interurban, it never owned or operated streamlined cars such as on the neighboring North Shore Line or the nearby Illinois Terminal. Here, one of the two streamlined Electroliners on the North Shore Line operates northbound past Pipers Road near Racine, Wisconsin, on a snowy winter day. LARRY PLACHNO.

When compared to the South Shore Line, the Chicago Aurora & Elgin had both positive and negative points.

Above: From the all-important aspect of revenue-producing freight, the South Shore Line was obviously superior. This photo shows the variety of South Shore Line freight equipment at their Michigan City, Indiana, shops on July 11, 1960. At the left can be seen a portion of South Shore #1012, an 80-ton steeple cab locomotive. In the center is #802, one of three South Shore "Little Joes," the largest locomotives ever operated by an interurban. To the rear, in the shop, is one of the 700-class locomotives, rebuilt by South Shore Line in their own shop from ex-New York Central locomotives. JAY LENTZNER / LARRY PLACHNO COLLECTION.

Below: South Shore #1126 was a 1908 Baldwin product built for the Chicago Lake Shore & South Bend. These early Lake Shore cars were heavy, powered by alternating current, and not as fast as the early Aurora Elgin & Chicago cars. LARRY PLACHNO COLLECTION.

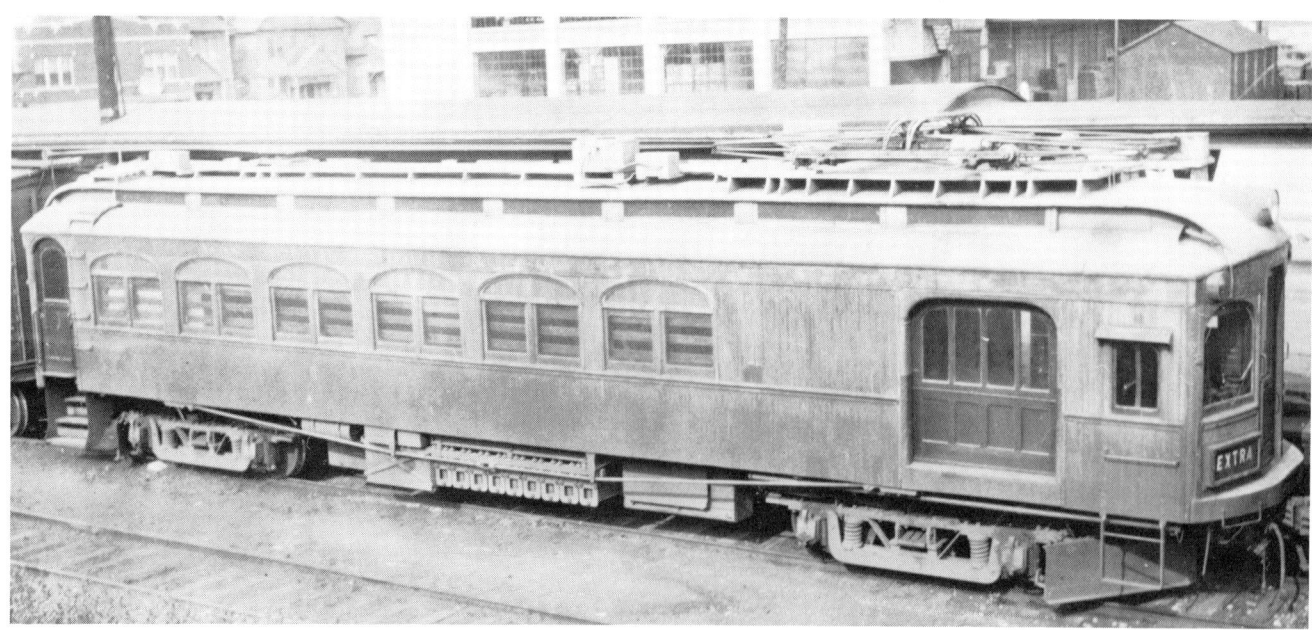

ed by Dr. Thomas Conway. Conway was well known and well regarded in the interurban industry at that time and his willingness to take over the CA&E spoke well for the railroad. Later that same decade, the CA&E came under the control of the Insull group whose holdings covered several major properties in the Midwest and isolated operations elsewhere. The involvement of these four groups not only did a great deal to mold the CA&E into the superior interurban it was, but they also insured financial stability and longevity for the line.

At least during the early years, the CA&E was superior to its neighbors in the area of equipment. The initial order of cars for the AE&C in 1902 was easily the most powerful, and probably fastest, interurban cars built up until that time. It is also interesting to note that the AE&C started out with cars that could operate over the elevated line into Chicago. Both the North Shore Line and the South Shore Line started out with equipment that was markedly inferior to what the AE&C was operating in 1902 as well as what they would later operate.

The CA&E achieved some stature from the standpoint of eliminating street operation. Due perhaps in part to its third rail power, the CA&E's main line from Chicago to Wheaton was built entirely on private right-of-way. Only the branches beyond Wheaton had any street operation where overhead trolley wires had to be used. By comparison, the original double track main lines of both the Chicago North Shore & Milwaukee and the Chicago South Shore & South Bend were built with extensive street trackage.

The majority of CA&E street operation was discontinued in 1937 with the abandonment of their West Chicago-Geneva-St. Charles branch. The remaining CA&E street operation was discontinued in 1939 with a trackage relocation in Aurora. By comparison, the Chicago North Shore & Milwaukee had street operation on its Shore Line Route and maintained street operation in Milwaukee until their respective dates of abandonment. The Chicago South Shore & South Bend still conducts street operation in Michigan City.

In addition, the CA&E achieved some stature by being the last of the Chicago interurbans to take delivery of interurban cars. In spite of the North Shore Line's placing two electric streamliners in service in 1941, the CA&E ordered ten somewhat conventional cars from the St. Louis Car Co. that same year. Because of the war, they were not delivered until late 1945. Clearly, the CA&E was planning on staying in the passenger business. The last conventional heavy interurban car was built for a Canadian line in 1948, making this CA&E car order one of the very last in the industry. We will leave it to the reader to decide whether the new South Shore Line cars, delivered in the early 1980's, should mitigate the CA&E's achievement in this regard.

Also, although the CA&E suffered a receivership in 1919, it could claim to be generally more profitable and more financially sound than the two other members of this Chicago trio. By comparison, the CA&E did not suffer from the many years of receivership and debts which plagued the Chicago North Shore & Milwaukee. And, had it not been for Samuel Insull, the Chicago Lake Shore & South Bend would have probably been abandoned and scrapped in the late 1920's.

Eight streamlined interurban cars for the Illinois Terminal were delivered in the late 1940's. In spite of the attractive cars, partronage declined and the company ceased interurban passenger service before these cars reached their tenth birthday.
LARRY PLACHNO COLLECTION.

Above: The North Shore Line was able to operate high-speed service from Chicago to Milwaukee after Insull control provided the new Skokie Valley Line in the 1920's. This double track high-speed right-of-way between Skokie and Lake Bluff included heavy rail and overhead catenary suspended from sturdy catenary bridges. Here, train No. 209 (cars 176-412-158-161-716) northbound between Woodridge and Briargate at 6:04 p.m., Wednesday, June 13, 1962. JOHN D. HORACHEK.

Below: The North Shore Line also had some local branch line service. Car #710, built by Cincinnati Car Co. in 1924, prepares to leave Lake Bluff for the short run to Mundelein. In many respects, the North Shore Line cars were very similar to those operated by the Chicago Aurora & Elgin. LARRY PLACHNO.

HOW THEY WERE DIFFERENT

Some things made the CA&E substantially different from the other two Chicago Insull interurbans. Other than some street, terminal, freight spur and shop trackage, the CA&E was powered by third rail. As far as is known, this was the only significant use of third rail power between Michigan and the West Coast other than Chicago's rapid transit operation. Although creating a potential safety hazard, the third rail provided an impression of heavy duty standards to the line and was somewhat in keeping with its frequent service.

The routes of the CA&E were very untypical of an interurban railroad. A double-track main line to Wheaton divided into two single-track branches, which in turn split into two more branches each. Hence the CA&E reached the Fox River at four points: Elgin, Geneva, Batavia, and Aurora. This provided a funnel-shaped route with Wheaton at the neck and Chicago at the base of the funnel. It appears that no other interurban electric railroad achieved a similar "funnel shaped" route structure. Because of this structure, the CA&E maintained a rather unusual operation with branch line cars coupling together or feeding into each other as they approached Chicago.

WHERE CA&E FELL BEHIND

Alas, the Chicago Aurora & Elgin was also inferior in some respects to the other two major Chicago interurbans. While both the North Shore Line and the South Shore Line were to win electric traction speed trophies, the CA&E spent much of its later life as a plodding commuter carrier. This does not imply that CA&E trains were particularly slow. Actually, in comparison with typical Indiana and Ohio interurbans the CA&E did quite well in the area of speed. However, both the CNS&M and the CSS&SB achieved some substantial prominence in the area of winning electric traction speed trophies. Most, if not all, of the CA&E cars could attain at least 65 (or even 70) miles per hour. But, the station stops were so close that CA&E cars rarely had an opportunity to build up speed except for a few long rural stretches on the single track branches. It is known that the CA&E made a good showing in some of the speed contests, usually with the Cannonball or similar non-stop trains, but was never able to take the top prizes.

In overall size, based on route miles, the CA&E was the smallest of the three Chicago Insull interurbans. Technically (exclusive of the Mt. Carmel and Westchester branches) the CA&E could claim a maximum length of 67 route miles, which did not include trackage rights over the Chicago rapid transit nor the one-time-affiliated Fox River lines. At one time or another, a small portion of this mileage was effectively operated by the Chicago rapid transit. After the abandonment of the Geneva branch in 1937, this route mileage (exclusive of the two smaller branches) was close to 56 miles.

Admittedly, the CA&E made up for its lack of route miles by providing frequent service. In its best years, the CA&E operated four trains per hour between Chicago and Wheaton, easily the most frequent interurban schedule in the Chicago area and possibly a record among all interurbans.

The CA&E also retained the dubious distinction of being one of the few railroads with minimal passenger car storage at its terminal points. The tiny Wells Street Terminal offered very little car storage and many rush hour cars were deadheaded back to the Lockwood yard at Laramie Avenue for mid-day storage. Both Elgin and Aurora offered only minimal car storage capacity. The change to the Forest Park terminal in 1953 did little to improve the car storage situation. Hence, Wheaton yards became the focal point for car storage as well as operations and maintenance. Because of this the CA&E suffered from having to move cars to and from Wheaton for car storage with many runs that carried few passengers. It might be noted that today the Chicago South Shore & South Bend continues to schedule a very early morning departure from Michigan City to South Bend for the same reason since they no longer store cars in South Bend.

The CA&E was the only one of the three major Chicago interurbans which did not build and benefit from a bypass route. In the mid-1920's the Insull management built the Skokie Valley Route for the North Shore Line. This route permitted competitive service from Illinois to Wisconsin and survived the slower Shore Line route by several years. The East Chicago bypass for the South Shore Line, originally planned by the Insull management, was finally installed in 1956. The Conway management did plan (or continue plans) on a bypass route for the CA&E from Bellwood through Westchester to the Aurora branch, but it was never completed beyond Westchester.

In the area of equipment, the CA&E was also behind its two contemporaries in one respect. Although the CA&E could lay claim to operating the newest equipment in the form of its St. Louis cars (at least until arrival of the new South Shore Line cars in the 1980's), it also operated the oldest. Until the end of passenger operations, the CA&E was still operating some wooden coaches in commuter service.

A major problem area for the CA&E, and perhaps a major reason for its earlier demise than its companion Chicago lines, was its inability to generate any substantial freight traffic. Parallel steam railroads and a lack of on-line industries precluded the CA&E from carrying as much freight as the other two major Chicago interurbans. Hence, the CA&E was doomed to being primarily a passenger and a commuter carrier, and suffered accordingly.

The CA&E had only six freight locomotives, all of relatively standard "juice jack" or "steeple cab" design. The companion North Shore Line eventually acquired two large electric locomotives for its freight. The South Shore Line purchased the three massive "Little Joe" locomotives (largest to operate on any interurban) and later rebuilt several large ex-New York Central locomotives for its own use. Unlike the CA&E and the North Shore Line, the South Shore Line survived because the revenue from its extensive freight business substantially overcame passenger deficits until the day of passenger subsidies arrived.

Of the three Chicago Insull interurbans, the CA&E was the first to suffer a major trackage abandonment.

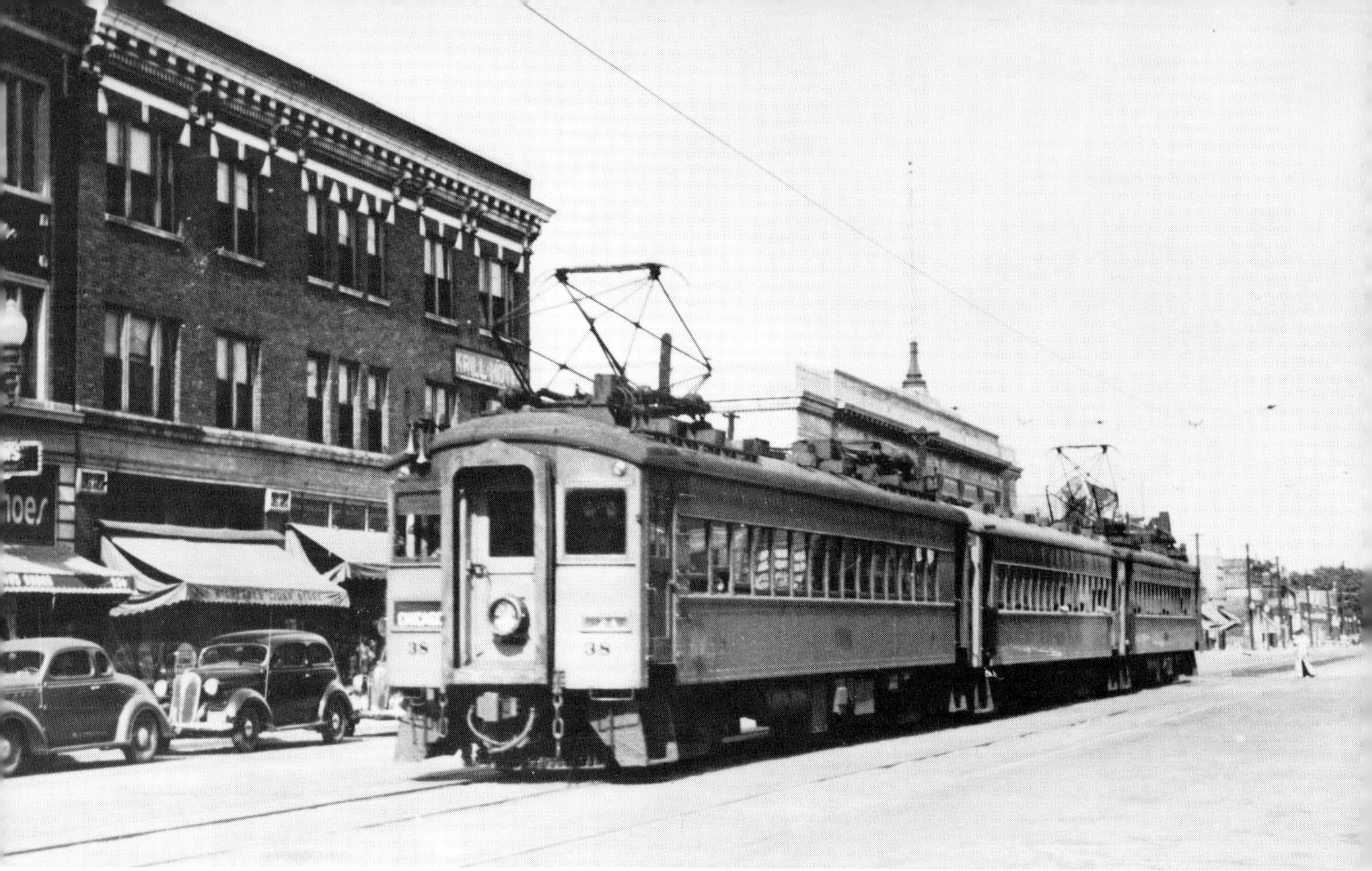

Above: The Chicago Aurora & Elgin was the only one of the three Chicago Insull interurbans to eliminate all street operation. At the time of abandonment in 1963, the North Shore Line was still operating on city streets in Milwaukee. The South Shore Line did eliminate street operation in South Bend and East Chicago but continues to operate on city streets in Michigan City. On July 23, 1939, a three-car train of South Shore Line cars operates through East Chicago. CHARLES A. BROWN.

Below: Very few segments of former interurban lines survived the Chicago Aurora & Elgin in passenger service. In July of 1959, while the CA&E was closing down its remaining freight operations, a transit authority was running the last remaining Pacific Electric passenger line from Los Angeles to Long Beach. Cars #1543-1524 are shown at the Los Angeles River crossing. This operation survived only two more years. CHARLES BYCROFT / LARRY PLACHNO COLLECTION.

This came in 1937 when the CA&E abandoned its Geneva branch. However, in support of this action it might be stated that the Geneva branch was built to a standard considerably inferior to the remainder of the railroad, and also had little patronage. This was in part due to the fact that it paralleled the C&NW main line from Wheaton to West Chicago and Geneva. Prior to this date, the only abandonments had been minor as the CA&E had removed only some street trackage in Aurora and the outer portion of its Mt. Carmel branch. By 1937 the South Shore Line had abandoned only two short branches, and the North Shore Line had removed only some street trackage and replaced some routes with new trackage.

Finally, the Chicago Aurora & Elgin had the unfortunate distinction of being the first of the Chicago Insull interurbans to suffer passenger declines and total abandonment. The CA&E abandoned passenger service in 1957, but trackage remained virtually intact until 1958 when the Batavia branch was severed for the new tollway, and 1959 when freight service ended. Technically, total abandonment of the CA&E did not come about until July of 1961 (only 1½ years before the North Shore Line).

Although this aspect of the CA&E was the poorest of the three major Chicago interurbans, it was excellent in regard to other interurbans. By 1932, half of all interurban mileage had been abandoned or had at least ceased passenger service. By 1959, only the North Shore Line and the South Shore Line were left operating significant interurban passenger service in the United States, and the North Shore Line ceased its operations in early 1963. Hence, the Chicago Aurora & Elgin achieved the distinction of being one of the last operating passenger interurban electric railways in the nation.

Although the North Shore Line never did obtain freight traffic and revenues to equal the South Shore Line, it did better than the Chicago Aurora & Elgin in this regard. North Shore Line #456 is shown during a switching movement at Pettibone yard in a heavy snow during the 1950's. This locomotive, a 1927 General Electric steeple cab of about 65 tons, was equipped with batteries so it could operate on non-electrified track for short periods. LARRY PLACHNO.

3

Wells Street Terminal

In 1905 the Aurora Elgin & Chicago made arrangements to use the Metropolitan West Side Elevated Railway tracks to reach Wells Street Terminal (then known as 5th Avenue Terminal) in downtown Chicago. Regular AE&C passenger service into the Wells Street Terminal began on March 8, 1905. Prior to this time the AE&C cars had terminated at Laramie Avenue and passengers to Chicago transferred to "L" trains.

Records indicate that some AE&C trains operated into Chicago over the Metropolitan "L" tracks prior to 1905 and that the agreement to eventually operate all trains into downtown Chicago dates from prior to the start of AE&C construction. The AE&C operated a newspaper train daily during the wee hours of the morning from Chicago to Fox River points as early as 1903. There are indications that a few special passenger movements operated into Chicago prior to 1905.

This 1905 trackage agreement to reach downtown Chicago was somewhat unique at this time and set several precedents. It appears to be the first occurrence of an interurban line operating over rapid transit tracks. It also was the first instance of an interurban line serving downtown Chicago directly.

The Wells Street Terminal was not particularly unusual at the time. Four different companies owned portions of the rapid transit lines emanating from Chicago's central business district. Each of these elevated companies had built a terminal on the edge of the central business district. The Wells Street Terminal was originally constructed by the Metropolitan West Side Elevated Railway, the company whose tracks the Aurora Elgin & Chicago used to reach Chicago. After the construction of the "Union Loop Elevated," the various elevated railways began routing their trains around the Loop and these various terminals on the edge of the business district became less and less important. Some of these terminals, like Wells Street, continued in use until well after World War II.

Located at 314 South Wells Street, between Jackson and Van Buren, the Wells Street Terminal was one of only three railroad stations to actually touch upon the outer perimeter of the Loop, and none ever managed to get inside its confines. Located in the southwest quadrant of the Loop, the Wells Street Terminal was but a short walk from Chicago's main financial district. The main shopping area was located on the opposite side of the Loop, but this could easily be reached by transfer to the "L" trains around the Loop. Actually, many suburban commuters simply preferred to walk across the Loop.

In basic design, the Wells Street Terminal consisted of four stub-end tracks on a typical "L" structure. Two center platforms served the four tracks. When initially constructed, the upper level of the Terminal was entirely open and all functions (including sale of AE&C tickets) were handled on one main level beneath the "L" structure.

In 1926, when Insull interests controlled both the CA&E and the elevated lines, substantial improvements were made at the Wells Street Terminal. Two additional levels were added between the end of track and the street. A new waiting room permitted passengers to walk directly out to the train platforms. A small bridge to the existing "L" structure (over Wells Street) permitted ease of transfer between CA&E trains and both elevated and North Shore Line trains.

In addition to passenger service, the Terminal also served as a major point for the acceptance and dispatch of CA&E's "Fast Package Service." This was sent and received on regular passenger trains. The CA&E also maintained some office space in the Terminal for use at various times by the General and Freight Agent, the Passenger Agent and Public Relations Staff.

During its last years of use, the Wells Street Terminal had grown to be a miniature version of a large railroad terminal. The busy ground floor contained a checkroom, telephones, a concession, a restaurant, and even a barber shop. Upstairs on the third floor were both the train concourse and the ticket office. Although small in size, the Wells Street Terminal at least made

---

PRECEDING PAGE

Official Chicago Rapid Transit photo of the Wells Street Terminal looking northwest along Wells Street. This shows work almost complete on the 2nd and 3rd story addition during the remodeling of 1926. CHICAGO RAPID TRANSIT / STEVE HYETT COLLECTION.

Above: Although the photo quality is not the best, it appears that the CA&E service was holding up well this day as four interurbans prepare to depart from all four tracks of the Wells Street Terminal. The photo was probably taken in the mid-1920's after the delivery of the new steel cars but before the terminal expansion. LARRY PLACHNO COLLECTION.

Below: Wells Street Terminal was a very busy place during the War when patronage increased substantially. Stephenson car #30 is on the back end of a 5-car train pulling out of the Wells Street Terminal. The year was 1941 and the wooden car had already seen nearly four decades of use. STEPHEN D. MAGUIRE / RICHARD ALLERMANN COLLECTION.

an attempt to offer many of the same services provided by the major steam railroads in their terminals.

Overall storage capacity in the terminal was rather small and operations became quite crowded during the rush hour when "L" trains also departed from the Terminal. The mid-day car storage problem was resolved by deadheading cars to and from the Lockwood coach yard, just west of Laramie Ave. In the earlier years, even the mid-day and weekend operations at Wells Street were substantial. Basic headway on the AE&C to Wheaton in those days was 15 minutes, which required a minimum of eight train movements per hour at the Terminal.

CA&E operations at Wells Street Terminal ended on September 20, 1953, when Des Plaines Avenue in Forest Park became the new eastern terminal. After midnight, car #421 headed the last CA&E train west out of the terminal for the last time.

The Terminal building itself did not survive for much longer. By 1955 the upper levels of the Terminal had been removed and the center two stub tracks lengthened to connect with the Loop "L" structure. In order to replace the former "L" connection with the Loop over Van Buren Street, Garfield Park "L" trains were then routed through the old Terminal and past the old platforms to get on the Loop trackage. This arrangement ended when the subway was extended to connect with the new median strip trackage on the Congress Expressway.

Wells St. Terminal

This overhead view shows both the platform and "throat" of Wells Street Terminal. In the foreground are the four platform tracks, all crowded with Chicago Aurora & Elgin cars. In the background, looking west, are the tracks leading to Market Street Junction. A CA&E train has just left the station headed for Wheaton or the Fox River Valley. ROBERT W. GIBSON.

Above: The throat to Wells Street Terminal ended here at what was often called Market Street Junction. Those tracks going straight ahead went to the Wells Street Terminal while those directly behind the photographer went west to Marshfield, Forest Park and Wheaton. The two tracks cutting off to the right carried "L" trains to the Loop elevated structure. WILLIAM C. JANSSEN.

Below: The Wells Street Terminal was nothing more than a conventional elevated structure. This view from street level on Franklin Street shows Chicago Surface Lines streetcar #1640 about to turn into the Van Buren tunnel under the Chicago River. CA&E cars in the Wells Street Terminal can be seen in the distance. WILLIAM E. ROBERTSON.

Above: Stephenson car #56 loads passengers at the Wells Street Terminal. Although wooden and steel cars were rarely mixed in the same train, they often operated side-by-side as in this photograph. GREG HEIER COLLECTION.

Below: This 1955 photo facing west shows the Wells Street facility after the terminal building had been torn down. The two center tracks will soon be extended to the Loop elevated structure to permit through operation of Garfield Park "L" trains and removal of the "L" structure on their former route over Van Buren Street. VIC WAGNER / RICHARD ALLERMANN COLLECTION.

Sunset Lines • 31

4

On The "L"

From 1905 to 1953, the cars of the Chicago Aurora & Elgin operated over Metropolitan West Side Elevated tracks in order to reach downtown Chicago. This agreement spanned nearly a half-century and witnessed corporate changes on both sides.

The original agreement of 1905 was made between the Aurora Elgin & Chicago and the Metropolitan West Side Elevated Railway. The Chicago elevated lines were later consolidated, shared Insull control with the CA&E for a period, and eventually became a transit authority. By 1953, the two participants in the trackage agreement were the Chicago Aurora & Elgin and the Chicago Transit Authority.

It is interesting to note that early records indicate that when AE&C trains started operating over the "L" into Chicago, cars stopped only at the 5th Avenue Terminal (Wells Street), Marshfield, and 52nd Avenue (Laramie). Additional stops on the "L" were added in later years.

A large measure of the CA&E's success and longevity was due to this relatively high-speed entrance into Chicago. Interurban railways were generally unable to build their own tracks into major cities. Most resorted to the use of local streetcar tracks, although a few lucky ones were able to use some existing railroad tracks. Had the CA&E been forced to enter Chicago on streetcar tracks, or been forced to transfer passengers to the "L," it most likely would not have survived the 1930's. As it was, the entrance to Chicago over the "L" not only provided CA&E passengers with a one-seat ride to Chicago's Loop, but also provided service which was fast enough to be competitive with private automobiles and nearby steam railroad commuter service.

PRECEDING PAGE

The big "S" curve just east of Halsted Street slowed down CA&E (and rapid transit) motormen because it required a speed restriction. However, for the photographer it was a unique location because of the four-track elevated curve and buildings in the background. Here, wood car #308, built by Niles, heads a westbound three-car limited. GREG HEIER COLLECTION.

For the most part, the "L" trackage was substantially compatible with CA&E's own tracks. Both used an over-running third rail and similar voltage. It was technically possible for "L" equipment to operate over CA&E trackage and for CA&E equipment to operate over the "L." The only real incompatability was that "L" cars required high-level platforms for passenger loading. All CA&E interurban passenger cars had traps over the stepwells which permitted loading at high level platforms when lowered, and loading at ground level when raised. The rapid transit cars, however, could only load at high level platforms. Some of the CA&E cars (particularly the ex-WB&A cars, which were not built with the "L" in mind) could have encountered minor clearance problems on certain parts of the "L" system. Although they apparently had no problem operating over the Garfield "L," the ex-WB&A cars were known to have encountered difficulties elsewhere on the "L" when on loan to the North Shore Line.

Operation of CA&E and rapid transit trains over each other's trackage was not particularly unusual. Both cooperated in operating a joint funeral service from points on the "L" to cemeteries on the CA&E. And there are numerous recorded occasions where CA&E, North Shore Line and the "L" borrowed cars from each other when the situation warranted. There were numerous outings of Chicago company "employee" picnics using rapid transit or "L" cars running on weekends to Glenwood Park in Batavia, "Home Seeker" trips to Ardmore (now Villa Park), and to downtown Aurora for transfer to streetcars on Broadway for the trip to Riverview/Fox River Park south of Aurora.

CA&E trains originated from the stub-end Wells Street Terminal on the perimeter of the Loop. Upon leaving the Terminal, westbound CA&E trains would go through the throat of the yard on a conventional "L" structure surrounded by office buildings. Within a few moments the trains would emerge beyond the buildings and approach an interlocking tower which controlled a junction with a two-track line from the south, by which "L" trains operated above Van Buren Street to reach the Loop.

Sunset Lines • 33

On the

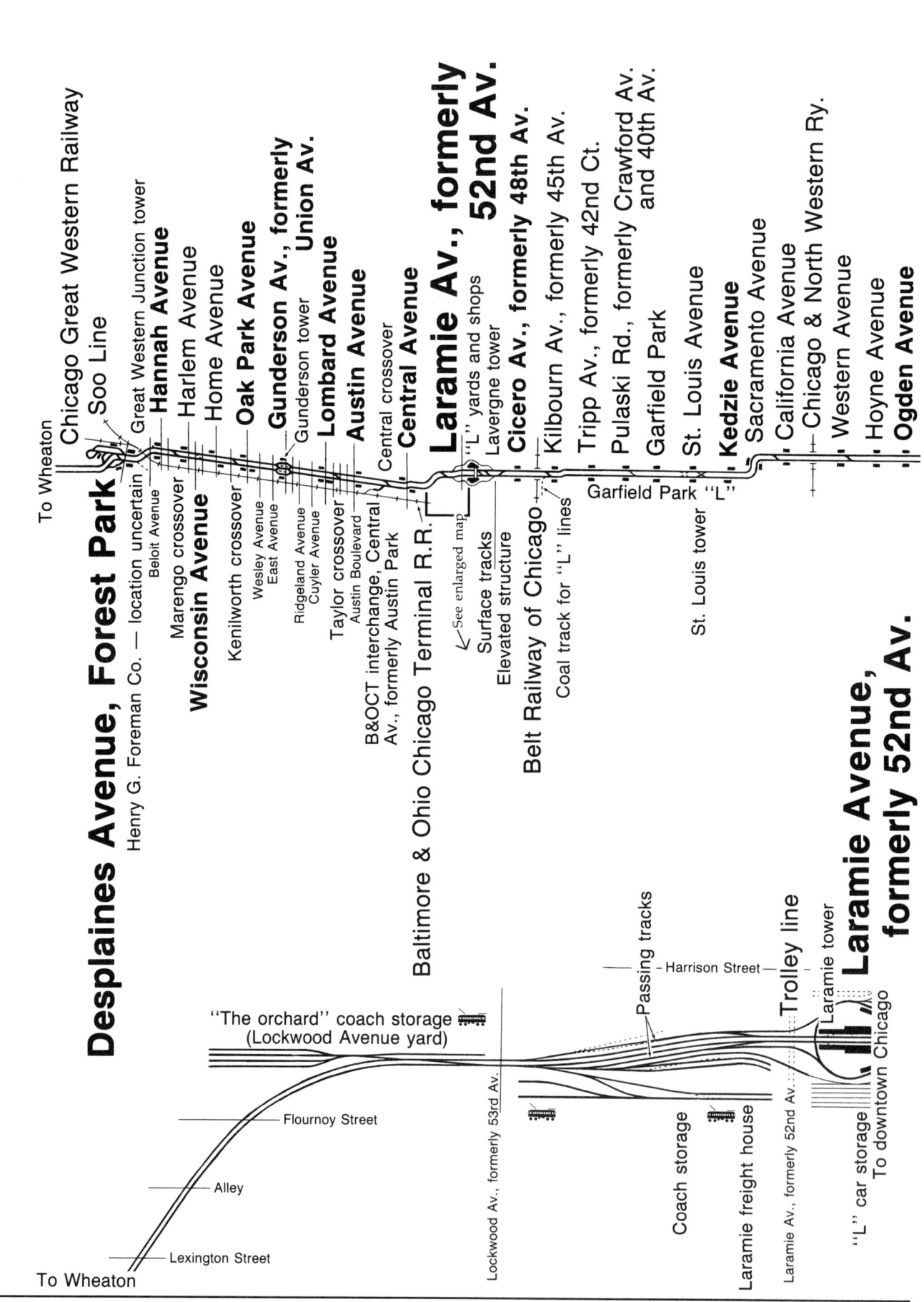

34 • Sunset Lines

"L"

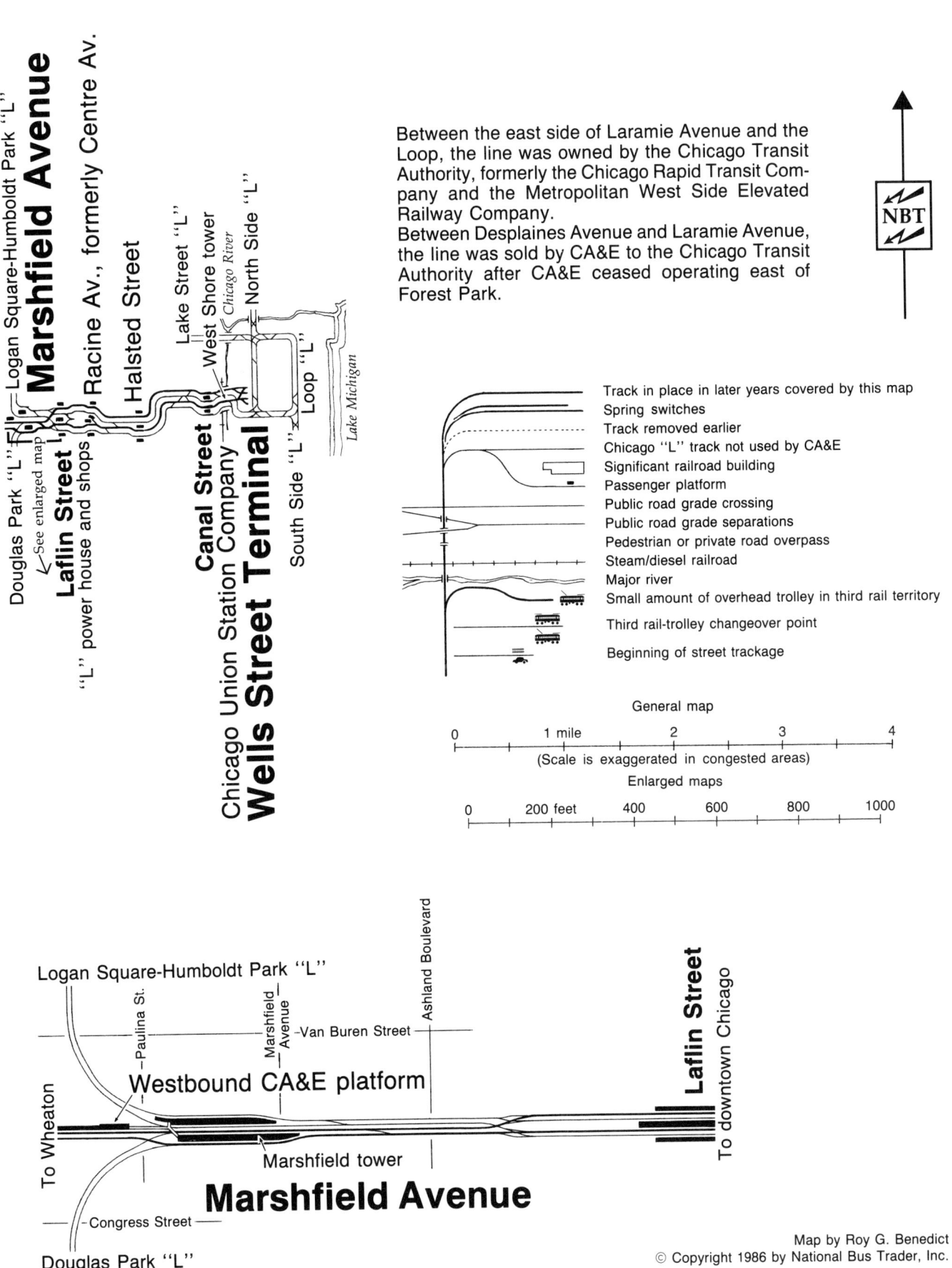

Between the east side of Laramie Avenue and the Loop, the line was owned by the Chicago Transit Authority, formerly the Chicago Rapid Transit Company and the Metropolitan West Side Elevated Railway Company.

Between Desplaines Avenue and Laramie Avenue, the line was sold by CA&E to the Chicago Transit Authority after CA&E ceased operating east of Forest Park.

Map by Roy G. Benedict
© Copyright 1986 by National Bus Trader, Inc.

Above: A 4-car evening rush hour train rolls through the Racine Avenue station in August of 1953. The "L" was still four tracks at this point but a small rapid transit shop facility was located between the center two tracks at this location. CA&E trains did not stop at Racine and we surmise that the passengers on the north platform are probably waiting for a Logan Square train. TRUMAN HEFNER / LARRY KOSTKA

Below: Marshfield was a major junction for the west side rapid transit. At this point the Logan Square (and Humboldt Park) service turned north, the Douglas Park service turned south (tracks turning to the left in photo), and the Garfield Park and CA&E trains continued straight ahead. Beyond this point the "L" structure was only two tracks. On September 6, 1953, buildings had been ripped down to make way for the new expressway. Pullman car #402 brings up the rear on a 4-car train at the CA&E's Marshfield platform while the Ogden Avenue stop can be seen in the distance. The CA&E was in the last month of operation on the "L" and the structure itself was due to be torn down soon. A. W. JOHNSON / RICHARD ALLERMANN COLLECTION.

On September 6, 1953, CA&E Pullman car #410 operates as a one-car train while crossing over the Pennsylvania Railroad tracks near Racine Street, between Western and California. Buildings have already been torn down to make way for the new expressway. A. W. JOHNSON / RICHARD ALLERMANN COLLECTION.

After the Wells St. Terminal lead and this two-track "L" line merged, the "L" structure became four tracks heading west. From this point to Marshfield, the CA&E trains normally used the express tracks. Almost immediately the tracks passed over the South Branch of the Chicago River, Union Station's covered train platforms, and into the Canal Street Station which was a regular CA&E stop. CA&E schedules provided only one minute of running time from Wells Street to Canal Street.

The four-track "L" continued west through several curves and rapid transit stations. CA&E trains passed rapid transit station platforms at Halsted, Racine (site of rapid transit shops on the "L") and Laflin, but did not stop. The next stop for the CA&E was at Marshfield, three minutes from Canal. The CA&E had its own platform here for westbound trains, which was just west of the rapid transit platforms and beyond the junction.

In earlier years, the Marshfield station was an important junction for the Metroplitan West Side Elevated. From this point the Douglas Park "L" trains branched south on their own two-track elevated structure. Logan Square "L" trains branched north from here on their two-track elevated structure which also carried passengers to the Humboldt Park branch. Westbound from here was a two-track "L" structure carrying Garfield Park "L" trains and CA&E trains.

Leaving Marshfield, CA&E trains had four minutes to reach their next stop at Kedzie. Intermediate rapid transit stops passed by included Ogden Ave., Hoyne, Western, California, and Sacramento, the latter located on an "S" curve.

The station after Kedzie, St. Louis Avenue, was equipped with a crossover on each side of the station.

Here, a CA&E train could pass a slow-moving "L" train while it was stopped at the station. Beyond St. Louis Avenue, rapid transit platforms bypassed by CA&E trains included Garfield Park (the station and the "L" line took its name from the nearby park of the same name), Pulaski Road, Kilbourne, and Cicero. In later years, some CA&E trains did stop at Cicero instead of Laramie. After crossing Lavergne Avenue, the tracks began a gradual descent from the "L" structure and reached street level just before the Laramie Avenue yard and station.

Laramie Avenue is located about 6 miles from Chicago's Loop and required 14-16 minutes running time on the CA&E from Wells Street. This was the traditional point where trackage changed ownership from rapid transit to CA&E. The Laramie Station was located on the east (rapid transit) side of the street. East and south of the station was a rather large rapid transit yard for the "L" plus a small shop and smaller yard to the north.

Leaving the station, trains crossed Laramie Avenue at grade under protection of crossing gates. At one time a West Towns streetcar line operated on Laramie and was crossed at the same time. There was no wire problem, however, since the streetcars used overhead trolley wire while the "L" and CA&E used third rail.

After crossing Laramie, the tracks made an elongated "S" turn to the south and crossed Lockwood Avenue. Here the CA&E maintained a freight house for LCL and milk cans, as well as a small yard for mid-day storage of commuter cars for which there was no room at Wells Street. The two-track line continued west at street level but on private right-of-way. Gate protection was provided at street crossings but platforms were all high-level to accommodate the "L" cars.

Sunset Lines • 37

Above: Niles car #205 heads a westbound 4-car rush hour train at the California Avenue station. This was not a stop for CA&E trains. Note that the follower is already closing in. GREG HEIER COLLECTION.

Below: St. Louis car #457 is operating as a single-car train as it negotiates the big curve at Sacramento. The lack of adjacent buildings leads one to believe that expressway construction is ready to start. WILLIAM C. JANSSEN.

Above: **A two-car train rolls at speed through the Kilbourn Avenue station in 1953. Cincinnati car #427 was the lead car.** EDWARD FRANK JR. / RICHARD ALLERMANN COLLECTION.

Below: **West of Cicero Avenue the elevated structure began dropping to street level like a long ramp which ended just east of Laramie. At Lavergne Avenue, the elevated tracks were already halfway to ground level. St. Louis car #454 brings up the rear on a three-car westbound train.** DANIEL E. FRIZANE COLLECTION.

Above: The rapid transit company maintained this large yard and an inspection shop just east of the Laramie station. A six-car CA&E train has just left the Laramie station and is headed east to Chicago. DANIEL E. FRIZANE COLLECTION.

Below: A westbound three-car train has just rolled into the Laramie Avenue stop. Cincinnati car #430 is in the lead. The ramp leading down from the elevated structure can be seen in the distance on both this photo and the one above. GREG HEIER COLLECTION.

The next station after Laramie was Central Avenue, which was not a stop for the CA&E. Soon after passing this you could see the CA&E's interchange with the B&OCT to the south. This was the easternmost carload freight interchange on the CA&E and it was given up in 1953 when the CA&E cut operations back to Forest Park.

Following Central Avenue, CA&E trains passed but did not stop at rapid transit stations at Austin and Lombard Avenue. Soon after this the Gunderson Avenue station was reached. This was not a stop for the CA&E, but a short extra track between the regular tracks was installed through the station area to permit CA&E trains to pass slow-moving "L" trains. Just beyond this, another West Towns streetcar line was crossed and then CA&E trains stopped at the Oak Park Station, only three minutes after leaving Laramie Avenue. Eastbound CA&E trains used a low-level platform at Oak Park while "L" trains used a high-level platform.

Continuing west, the tracks remained relatively straight for a while, passing rapid transit platforms at Harlem and Hamlin, and then made a sweeping "S" curve to the south to cross the double railroad tracks used by several railroads, including the Chicago Great Western and the Soo Line. This crossing was at grade and conflicting movements necessitated holding CA&E or "L" trains until the crossing was clear. The CA&E was the "junior" railroad at this crossing which frequently caused major delays to both interurban and "L" trains. At Des Plaines Avenue in Forest Park, approximately 3 minutes beyond Oak Park Avenue, another set of streetcar tracks belonging to West Towns Railway were crossed.

As with the Wells Street Terminal, the "L" trackage lasted only briefly after the CA&E quit running on it. The last CA&E train rolled over the "L" after midnight on September 20, 1953. Within hours, one track was cut over to the temporary trackage on ground level along Van Buren Street. The other track followed in a few days. Soon after this, much of the "L" structure was torn down to make way for the new expressway. On June 22, 1958, rapid transit trains began using the new expressway trackage east of Forest Park which totally replaced the older trackage previously described above.

West of Central Avenue the CA&E maintained an interchange with the Baltimore & Ohio Chicago Terminal. This was the easternmost point for CA&E freight operation. Here locomotives #2001-2002 are switching the B&OCT interchange in 1951. CA&E's double track main line can be seen at the right. D. ST. CLAIR / RICHARD ALLERMANN COLLECTION.

Just slightly west of Laramie Avenue, the CA&E had their four-track Lockwood yard for mid-day storage of rush hour trains. A lack of storage space at Wells Street required that certain rush hour equipment be deadheaded to and from this point. Pullman #418 and Cincinnati #431 seem to be the guests at Lockwood yard on this particular occasion. GREG HEIER COLLECTION.

Above: April of 1951 found Cincinnati car #428 bringing up the rear on a CA&E train at Gunderson Avenue. The trackage arrangement here was unique in that it provided a center passing track so that faster interurban trains could get around the slower rapid transit trains. TRUMAN HEFNER / LARRY KOSTKA COLLECTION.

Below: St. Louis car #459 brings up the rear on a three-car westbound train at Oak Park Avenue. The low level platform on the left was used by eastbound CA&E trains to discharge passengers at Oak Park Avenue. Eastbound rapid transit trains used a high level platform on the other side of Oak Park Avenue. DANIEL E. FRIZANE COLLECTION.

Above: On August 6, 1941, a two-car CA&E train was headed west near Harlem Avenue with Jewett car #319 on the back end. On the right is the track of the Chicago Great Western. That little section of third rail in the left foreground was most frequently used to announce trains by ringing a bell at the next station up the line to warn passengers that a train was approaching. R. J. ANDERSON / RICHARD ALLERMANN COLLECTION.

Below: Just east of Des Plaines Avenue, CA&E and rapid transit trains had to cross the tracks of the Soo Line at grade. An interlocking tower controlled the crossing and the long Soo Line freight trains frequently played havoc with CA&E and rapid transit schedules. In November of 1951 an eastbound CA&E car is seen at this point. The interlocking tower can be seen to the right. TRUMAN HEFNER / GREG HEIER COLLECTION.

5

Forest Park

Forest Park is located about 9 miles west of Chicago's Loop. On the CA&E, the travel time from Wells Street Terminal to the Des Plaines Avenue Station in Forest Park was approximately 22 minutes. Although generally a significant point on the CA&E, its reason for importance changed several times, depending on train routings.

From the start of AE&C service in 1902 until 1905, the Forest Park Station was served entirely by the AE&C and it assumed no special importance.

With the 1905 mutual trackage agreement, Garfield Park "L" trains were extended to Forest Park and turned back at this point. A loop was provided for rapid transit trains just west of the Forest Park station. AE&C trains made regular stops west of Forest Park, but east of here they were restricted to only discharging passengers on eastbound trips and only picking up passengers on westbound trips. No local passengers were carried by CA&E trains east of Forest Park.

This situation changed again in 1926 when the "L" extended service west to Bellwood and Westchester over CA&E trackage. The CA&E continued to serve Forest Park but service was restricted east of Bellwood in deference to the "L." This was the only period in which both the CA&E and the "L" operated east and west of Forest Park.

Once again, in 1951, the situation changed when the Chicago Transit Authority discontinued rapid transit service on the Westchester branch and Forest Park became the western terminal for the "L" once more.

In 1953, the CA&E discontinued both passenger and freight service east of Forest Park and reverted to a transfer to "L" trains. A rather elaborate platform arrangement was constructed at Forest Park for this purpose consisting of one loop inside another loop. The CA&E, coming from the west, had the inner loop while CTA trains from the east had the outer loop. The CTA loop did cross over the CA&E lead tracks on a small bridge so that there would be no conflict in train movements. In turn, the CA&E loop crossed over the automobile entrance to the parking lot located in the center of the loops.

Two passenger platforms were provided between the CA&E and CTA tracks, one for westbound passengers and one for eastbound passengers. Hence, passengers transferring between the two had a simple across-the-platform transfer.

Normal procedure called for the CA&E trains to pull into the arrival platform and discharge passengers. Here they could walk across the platform to board a Chicago Transit Authority rapid transit train for Chicago. Then, the CA&E trains would circle around to the westbound departure platform. CTA passengers from Chicago would arrive at this same platform and could walk across to the CA&E trains.

Although a short storage track was provided, train operations were very constricted at this location. It became virtually impossible for one train to pass another at Forest Park. As a result, schedules were designed so as to permit trains to depart in their order of arrival. This was not a major problem for the CA&E since service was reduced substantially after 1953. Except for rush hours, there normally was only one train at a time in the Forest Park terminal. As had been the situation at Wells Street, it became necessary to run most trains back west for storage. Wheaton became the only significant car storage location after 1953.

After the end of CA&E passenger service, the CTA modified the Forest Park trackage to eliminate the CA&E loop, reduce the size of the CTA loop, and make the eastbound and westbound platforms parallel. For a while, a single CA&E track was maintained adjacent to the westbound platform for the possibility of resumption of service by CA&E. In effect, this would have given the CA&E a single track stub terminal which would have been very crowded for any substantial number of train movements.

PRECEDING PAGE

After September of 1953, Chicago Aurora & Elgin service was cut back to a new eastern terminal at Forest Park. Here the interurban cars transferred passengers to the rapid transit trains of the Chicago Transit Authority so that passengers could continue their trip to downtown Chicago. A Cincinnati steel car, #424, was on the rear of a train leaving the arrival platform and turning back west to the departure platform at Forest Park. DANIEL E. FRIZANE.

Above: This view was taken looking east from the end of the old Forest Park platform. Pullman #413 heads a westbound 4-car train while the follower appears to be closing in. The date was July 8, 1953, and rapid transit trains no longer went west of Forest Park while CA&E trains were in their last months of operating on rapid transit tracks. T. L. MCCONNELL COLLECTION.

Below: This early photo shows Niles car #203 on the old turning loop at Des Plaines Avenue. The loop was normally used to turn rapid transit trains to head back to Chicago. GREG HEIER COLLECTION.

1347 76

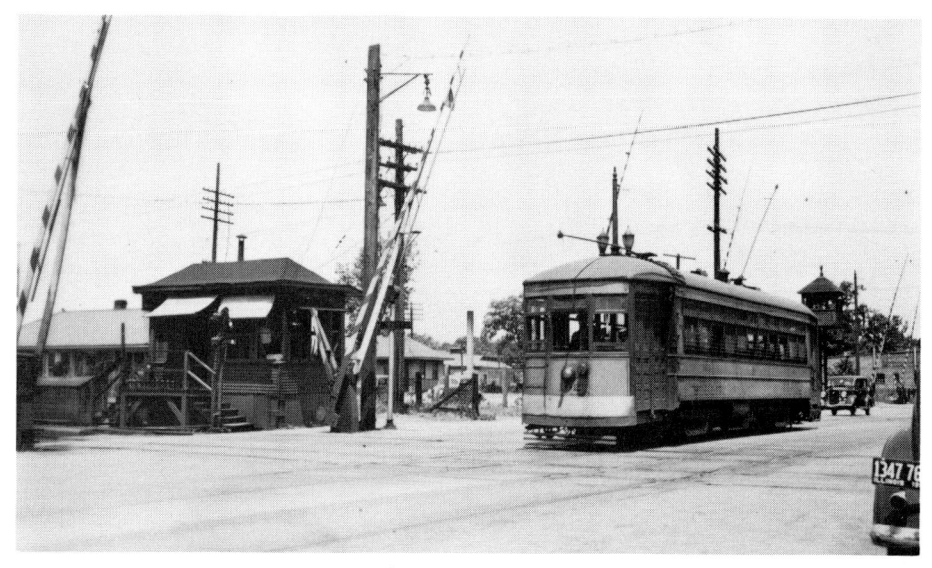

This early view looks northwest on Des Plaines Avenue and shows the multiple crossings prior to any grade separation. The first crossing was the CA&E/Rapid Transit, second was the Chicago Great Western, and third was the Soo Line. West Towns Railway car #102 was in the midst of negotiating this "obstacle course." FRANK KREJCIK / RICHARD ALLERMANN COLLECTION.

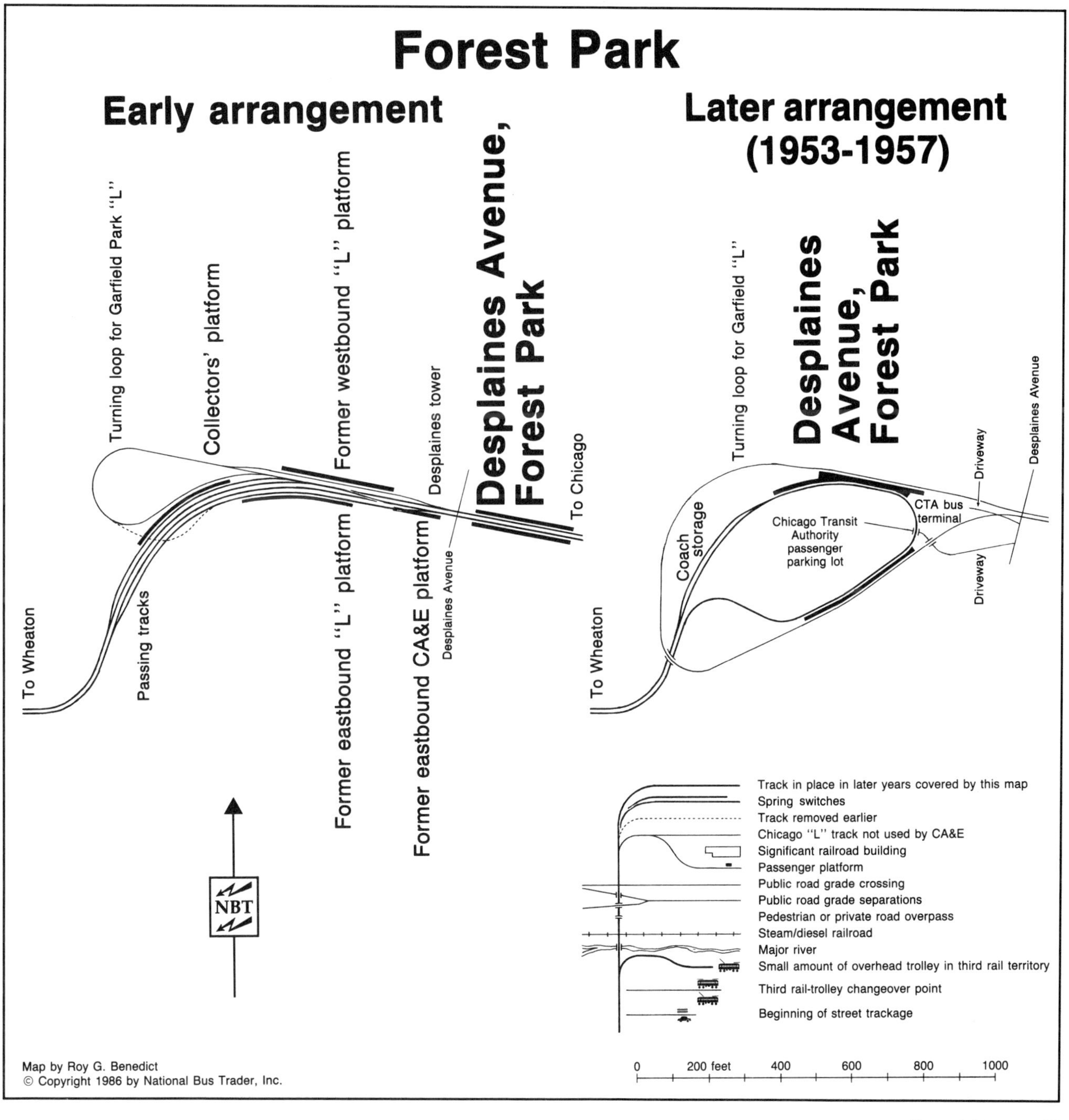
Forest Park
Early arrangement
Turning loop for Garfield Park "L"
Collectors' platform
Former westbound "L" platform
Desplaines tower
Desplaines Avenue, Forest Park
To Chicago
To Wheaton
Passing tracks
Former eastbound "L" platform
Former eastbound CA&E platform
Desplaines Avenue
Later arrangement (1953-1957)
Turning loop for Garfield "L"
Desplaines Avenue, Forest Park
Desplaines Avenue
Driveway
CTA bus terminal
Chicago Transit Authority passenger parking lot
Coach storage
Driveway
To Wheaton
NBT
Track in place in later years covered by this map
Spring switches
Track removed earlier
Chicago "L" track not used by CA&E
Significant railroad building
Passenger platform
Public road grade crossing
Public road grade separations
Pedestrian or private road overpass
Steam/diesel railroad
Major river
Small amount of overhead trolley in third rail territory
Third rail-trolley changeover point
Beginning of street trackage
Map by Roy G. Benedict
© Copyright 1986 by National Bus Trader, Inc.
0
200 feet
400
600
800
1000

Above: This shows the new terminal facility at Des Plaines Avenue after 1953. Pullman car #404 is discharging passengers on the eastbound platform. That little bridge just under the front of the car allowed cars to get under the CA&E track to reach the center parking lot. T. L. MCCONNELL COLLECTION.

Below: St. Louis car #457 leads a train around from the eastbound arrival platform (seen at the rear of the train) to the westbound departure platform. The photographer indicates that this was taken on a cold, cloudy morning in November of 1955. Note the sign on the bottom left directing passengers to CTA and CA&E trains. DONALD R. KAPLAN / SHORE LINE INTERURBAN HISTORICAL SOCIETY.

Above: **Immediately west of the CA&E westbound departure platform was a short siding for the storage of equipment. On this morning in November of 1955 we see five cars on the siding, including two ex-WB&A cars. The storage was obviously inadequate and CA&E ran most rush hour equipment back to Wheaton for mid-day storage.** DONALD R. KAPLAN / SHORE LINE INTERURBAN HISTORICAL SOCIETY.

Below: **A two-car Wheaton Express train consisting of St. Louis car #460 and Pullman car #407 round the loop at the Des Plaines Avenue terminal in November of 1955. One of the older rapid transit cars can be seen in the background.** DONALD R. KAPLAN.

6

Double Track Through Suburbia

Perhaps the best remembered segment of the Chicago Aurora & Elgin, and certainly the best patronized, was the double track main line between Forest Park and Wheaton. This portion of the interurban always had the most frequent headways and served the communities with the greatest populations.

Due in large part to the foresight and financial backing of the AE&C's founders, this portion of the line was substantially superior to most other interurbans. The double-track main line was powered by third rail and entirely on private right-of-way. In many respects, this double-track speedway of the CA&E resembled a major railroad electrification rather than an interurban. There were numerous street crossings at grade but most were protected by crossing gates while lesser streets were protected by conventional blinking crossing signals. There were portions of the line which had grade separated crossings with roads and other railroads.

Upon leaving Forest Park westbound, trains crossed over the Des Plaines River and then passed through a small industrial area with several sidings. Upon reaching the outskirts of Maywood, the CA&E began running parallel and immediately south of the tracks of the Chicago Great Western Railroad. The first stop beyond Forest Park, and main stop for Maywood, was Fifth Avenue. This was located approximately 2 miles west or 3-4 minutes from Forest Park. Continuing on, the CA&E's tracks remained parallel to the CGW through Maywood. Local stops were located at 11th Avenue and 17th Avenue in Maywood. Between 1926 and 1951, when the rapid transit operated west of Forest Park, these two stops were served exclusively by rapid transit trains and were bypassed by CA&E trains. After 1951, these two stops were served by most CA&E trains except for the limiteds destined for points beyond Wheaton. It is interesting to note that this may be the only situation on record where an interurban replaced rapid transit service.

Next was the stop at 25th Avenue in Bellwood. This had been served by both the rapid transit and CA&E prior to 1951, and reverted exclusively to the CA&E after that date. As late as the 1940's some CA&E limited trains stopped at 25th Avenue, but after 1953 it was served almost exclusively by local trains.

Continuing west, the CA&E tracks passed under the Indiana Harbor Belt line. This was originally a crossing at grade which caused frequent delays to CA&E schedules. The overpass for the IHB was built in 1931, easing operations for both the CA&E and IHB. Just beyond the IHB, the CA&E tracks crossed over Addison Creek, ran past the old IHB interchange, and then arrived at the Bellwood Avenue station.

Bellwood was approximately 4 miles or 7 minutes west of Forest Park by interurban. During most of the CA&E's life, Bellwood was a major junction and connecting point. From 1906 to 1926, a connection could be made at Bellwood with an AE&C shuttle car which meandered down the trolley-wire branch to Oak Ridge and Mt. Carmel Cemeteries. The Mt. Carmel shuttle car would normally wait for main line trains on a little stub track just south of the station.

From 1926 to 1951, the "L" extended service to Bellwood and down the Westchester branch which diverged at a double-track junction just east of the CA&E's Bellwood station. The rapid transit maintained its own Bellwood station immediately southeast of the CA&E station. During this period, CA&E trains stopped only at Bellwood Avenue, 25th Avenue, and 5th Avenue to receive passengers westbound and discharge passengers eastbound. By 1953, the Bellwood station had declined in importance and was bypassed by most limited trains. Stations east of Bellwood had high-level platforms for "L" cars.

PRECEDING PAGE

June 21, 1947 found St. Louis car #452 on the back of a four-car train headed east to Chicago. The photographer was facing east at the IHB crossing towards the 25th Avenue station in Bellwood. On the right is the old Jefferson Electric Co. siding while the Chicago Great Western right-of-way is obvious to the left. E. VAN DUSEN / RICHARD ALLERMANN COLLECTION.

Sunset Lines • 51

Double track

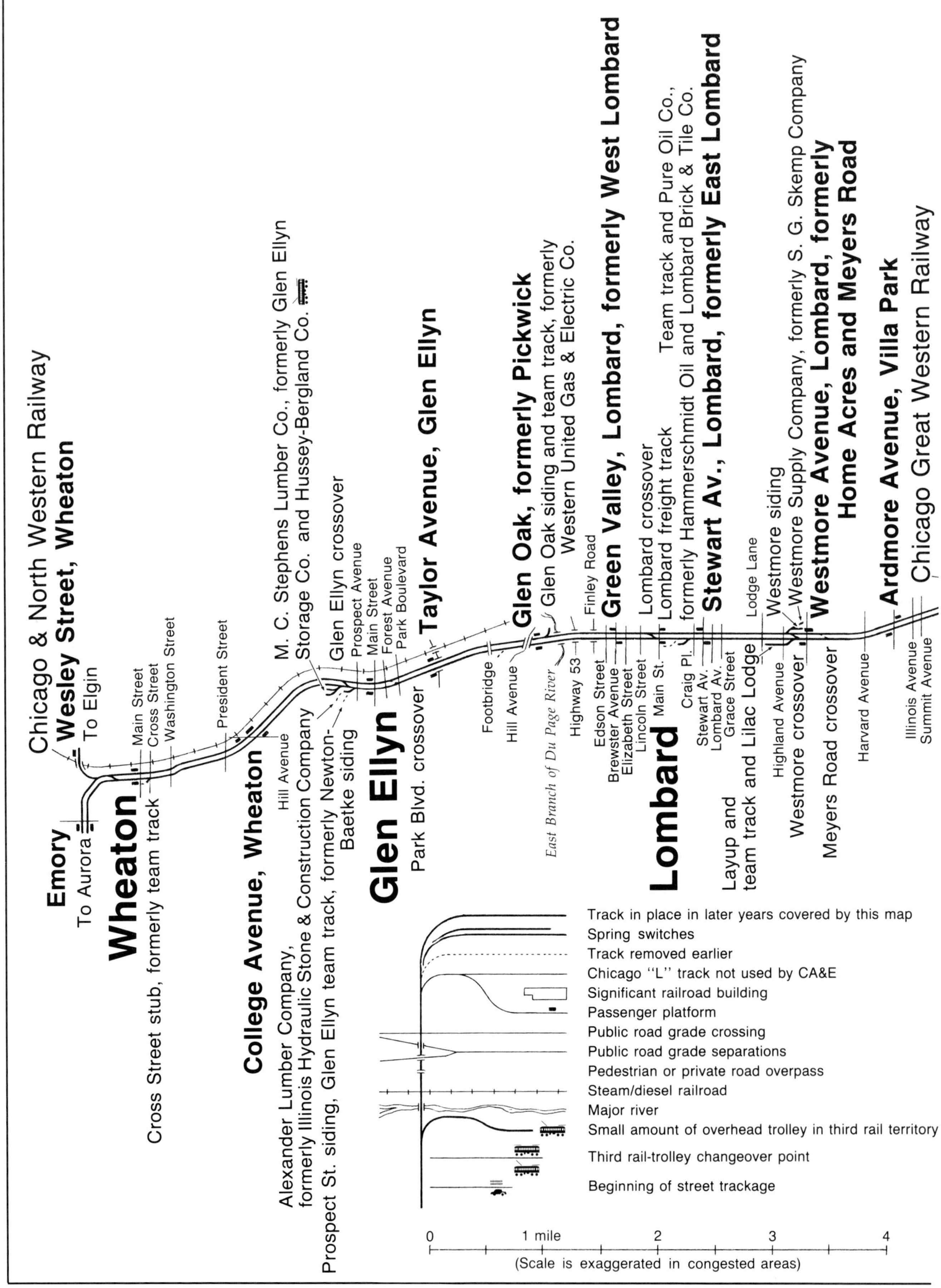

Emory
To Aurora

Chicago & North Western Railway
Wesley Street, Wheaton
To Elgin

Wheaton
Cross Street stub, formerly team track
Main Street
Cross Street
Washington Street
President Street

College Avenue, Wheaton
Hill Avenue
Alexander Lumber Company, formerly Illinois Hydraulic Stone & Construction Company
Prospect St. siding, Glen Ellyn team track, formerly Newton-Baetke siding
M. C. Stephens Lumber Co., formerly Glen Ellyn Storage Co. and Hussey-Bergland Co.
Glen Ellyn crossover
Prospect Avenue
Main Street
Forest Avenue
Park Boulevard

Glen Ellyn
Park Blvd. crossover

Taylor Avenue, Glen Ellyn
Footbridge
Hill Avenue

East Branch of Du Page River

Glen Oak, formerly Pickwick
Glen Oak siding and team track, formerly Western United Gas & Electric Co.
Finley Road
Highway 53
Edson Street
Brewster Avenue
Elizabeth Street
Lincoln Street

Green Valley, Lombard, formerly West Lombard
Lombard crossover
Lombard freight track formerly Hammerschmidt Oil and Lombard Brick & Tile Co.
Team track and Pure Oil Co.

Lombard
Main St.
Craig Pl.
Stewart Av.
Lombard Av.
Grace Street

Stewart Av., Lombard, formerly East Lombard
Layup and team track and Lilac Lodge
Lodge Lane
Westmore siding
Highland Avenue
Westmore crossover
Westmore Supply Company, formerly S. G. Skemp Company

Westmore Avenue, Lombard, formerly Home Acres and Meyers Road
Meyers Road crossover
Harvard Avenue

Ardmore Avenue, Villa Park
Illinois Avenue
Summit Avenue
Chicago Great Western Railway

Legend:
- Track in place in later years covered by this map
- Spring switches
- Track removed earlier
- Chicago "L" track not used by CA&E
- Significant railroad building
- Passenger platform
- Public road grade crossing
- Public road grade separations
- Pedestrian or private road overpass
- Steam/diesel railroad
- Major river
- Small amount of overhead trolley in third rail territory
- Third rail-trolley changeover point
- Beginning of street trackage

0 — 1 mile — 2 — 3 — 4
(Scale is exaggerated in congested areas)

52 • Sunset Lines

through Suburbia

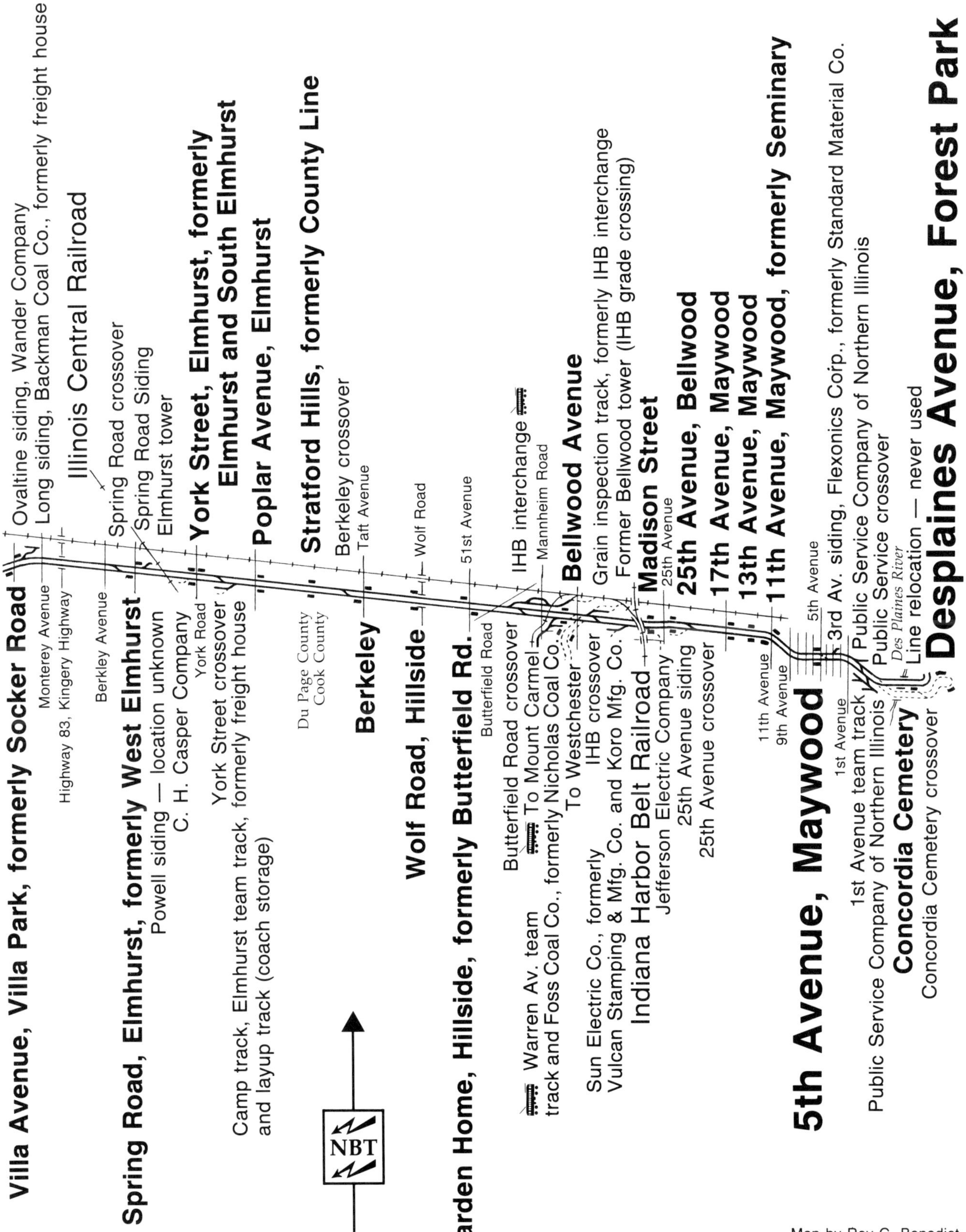

Villa Avenue, Villa Park, formerly Socker Road
— Ovaltine siding, Wander Company
— Long siding, Backman Coal Co., formerly freight house
— Monterey Avenue
— Highway 83, Kingery Highway

Illinois Central Railroad

Spring Road, Elmhurst, formerly West Elmhurst
— Berkley Avenue
— Spring Road crossover
— Spring Road Siding
— Elmhurst tower
— Powell siding — location unknown
— C. H. Casper Company
— York Road

York Street, Elmhurst, formerly Elmhurst and South Elmhurst
— York Street crossover
— Camp track, Elmhurst team track, formerly freight house and layup track (coach storage)

Poplar Avenue, Elmhurst

Stratford Hills, formerly County Line
— Du Page County / Cook County
— Berkeley crossover

Berkeley
— Taft Avenue

Wolf Road, Hillside
— Wolf Road
— 51st Avenue

Garden Home, Hillside, formerly Butterfield Rd.
— Butterfield Road
— Butterfield Road crossover
— To Mount Carmel
— Warren Av. team track and Foss Coal Co., formerly Nicholas Coal Co.
— To Westchester

IHB interchange
— Mannheim Road
— IHB crossover
— Sun Electric Co., formerly Vulcan Stamping & Mfg. Co. and Koro Mfg. Co.

Indiana Harbor Belt Railroad
— Jefferson Electric Company
— 25th Avenue siding
— 25th Avenue crossover
— Grain inspection track, formerly IHB interchange
— Former Bellwood tower (IHB grade crossing)

Bellwood Avenue

Madison Street
— 25th Avenue

25th Avenue, Bellwood

17th Avenue, Maywood

13th Avenue, Maywood

11th Avenue, Maywood, formerly Seminary
— 11th Avenue
— 9th Avenue

5th Avenue, Maywood
— 5th Avenue
— 1st Avenue
— 1st Avenue team track
— 3rd Av. siding, Flexonics Corp., formerly Standard Material Co.
— Public Service Company of Northern Illinois
— Public Service crossover
— Des Plaines River
— Line relocation — never used

Concordia Cemetery
— Public Service Company of Northern Illinois
— Concordia Cemetery crossover

Desplaines Avenue, Forest Park

↑ NBT

Map by Roy G. Benedict
© Copyright 1986 by National Bus Trader, Inc.

Sunset Lines • 53

Above: For several years, CA&E tracks between Forest Park and Bellwood were shared with Chicago Rapid Transit trains. The combination of the two companies provided very frequent service on this double-track stretch. In 1934, a 2300 series wooden passenger trailer and a 2900 series wooden passenger motor of the Chicago Rapid Transit company has just crossed the Des Plaines River bridge immediately west of Forest Park. RICHARD ALLERMANN COLLECTION.

Below: The CA&E's main stop for Maywood was located at 5th Avenue. In April of 1946, a six-car evening commuter train heads westbound. Note the flap at the end of the high level platforms to permit passage of conventional railroad cars.
WILLIAM C. JANSSEN / RICHARD ALLERMANN COLLECTION.

Above: **The 17th Avenue station was located on the west side of Maywood and was served exclusively by the rapid transit trains between 1926 and 1951. Westbound Cincinnati car #424 is seen passing through the station. Behind the station is the Chicago Great Western right-of-way.** GREG HEIER COLLECTION.

Below: **Passenger service had nearly ended in March of 1957 when Pullman car #406 headed a two-car train at the Bellwood station. The interlocking tower on the left formerly controlled the junction with the Westchester branch which cut off to the south at this point.** ROBERT W. GIBSON / LARRY KOSTKA COLLECTION.

Sunset Lines • 55

Above: Car #405 brings up the rear of a 2-car westbound train at Bellwood on March 10, 1957. To the left is the stub track formerly used by the shuttle car on the Cook County/Mt. Carmel branch. VICTOR G. WAGNER.

Below: Just west of the Bellwood station, the CA&E tracks crossed busy Mannheim Road. This photo looks west from that crossing on March 14, 1931. The CGW tracks are obvious to the north. GREG HEIER COLLECTION.

In later years, the interchange with the Indiana Harbor Belt line was located on the north side of the right-of-way and just west of Mannheim Road. On July 11, 1948, a 5-car train heads west on the main line while locomotives #3003-3004 switch the IHB interchange. GORDON E. LLOYD / LARRY PLACHNO COLLECTION.

Just west of Bellwood, tracks passed over the IHB track at grade and passed just south of the new IHB interchange. When freight service was discontinued, the IHB used this track to take over CA&E freight operations on the Mt. Carmel branch. The next stop for the CA&E was at Garden Home, located at 51st Avenue in Hillside. It was served mainly by the local trains.

Tracks continued west to pass over Wolf Road on an overpass where a stop of the same name was located. From there the next stop was at Berkeley, located at Taft Avenue. Both the Wolf Road and Berkeley stops were served mainly by the local trains.

Once past Berkeley, CA&E trains left Cook County and entered prosperous Du Page County. A stop called Stratford Hills had once been located at the county line. This stop was discontinued during the later years of World War II, most likely due to insufficient patronage and the growing importance of the Poplar Avenue stop.

The next community was Elmhurst, traditionally the largest community on the CA&E between Maywood and the Fox River. The first Elmhurst stop was at Poplar Avenue. This was a relatively new but local stop, having been put in during the 1930's. Slightly west was the York Road stop, which had been in place since the day the railroad started operating and was usually considered one of the two main stops in Elmhurst. On schedules after 1953, York Road in Elmhurst was usually the first stop for limited trains beyond Maywood and was listed as a stop on all schedules except the most important limiteds. It might be remembered that limited schedules after 1953 were making the same stops the old expresses had made. Prior to 1950, all Elmhurst and Villa Park stops were served by the local and express trains and only a few limiteds would stop.

Just west of York Road was the Illinois Central crossing at grade. This was the same track which crossed the Mt. Carmel branch and also interchanged with the Elgin branch at Elgin Junction.

The next stop was Spring Road in Elmhurst, the second of the two important stops in Elmhurst. Spring Road was approximately 17 miles from Chicago's Loop and required about 34 minutes of running time on a mid-day express schedule. In addition to being a relatively important stop, Spring Road had a small siding on the north side of the tracks which was used as a passing siding for evening westbound trains as late as the 1940's. People usually think of "meets" as involving trains in opposite directions on single track. The Chicago Aurora & Elgin, always being different, had meets between trains running in the same direction on double track.

Above: **Stephenson-built car #38 heads a westbound three-car train across Wolf Road, approaching the Wolf Road stop. The CGW tracks are obvious in the background.** DANIEL E. FRIZANE COLLECTION.

Below: **The new Poplar Avenue station in Elmhurst was recorded by the CA&E official photographer shortly after it was constructed. The date is November 28, 1931.** SHORE LINE INTERURBAN HISTORICAL SOCIETY / JACK R. BAILEY.

Above: The setting sun is in the motorman's eyes as he takes an evening commuter run through the Spring Road station in Elmhurst. Situations such as this undoubtedly brought about the nickname "Sunset Lines." WILLIAM E. ROBERTSON COLLECTION.

Below: The Villa Avenue station was generally considered to be the main stop in Villa Park. Here, westbound St. Louis car #455 crosses Villa Avenue. The station is on the left. WILLIAM C. JANSSEN / ERIC BRONSKY COLLECTION.

Above: **A two-car train of St. Louis cars is eastbound on the main line between Ardmore and Villa Avenue. The water tower in the distance marks the Villa Avenue station.** WILLIAM E. ROBERTSON COLLECTION.

Below: **The Ardmore Avenue station on the west side of Villa Park as it appeared after passenger service ended. This view looks west from the Ardmore Avenue crossing.** GREG HEIER.

Chicago Aurora & Elgin passenger service was in its final months of operation on March 27, 1957, when Pullman #417 headed this eastbound two-car train. The train is crossing Meyers Road at the Westmore station. VICTOR G. WAGNER

The CA&E was faced with a problem when the first limited and first express leaving Chicago after 5:00 p.m. on weekdays started catching up to the last sections of the Cannonball, which left Chicago just before 5:00 p.m. The solution was for the slower train to take the siding at Spring Road to let not one, but two fast trains pass. A similar meet was also planned further west at Westmore. This interesting arrangement ended in the early 1950's.

Beyond Elmhurst, the tracks rose up on an earth embankment to cross over Salt Creek and Highway 83, and turned away from the CGW tracks in a slightly more southwesterly direction. The CA&E paralleled the CGW tracks all the way from Maywood to just west of Highway 83. In actuality, the CGW was a good and welcome neighbor since it ran very little passenger service and could not be called a commuter line.

From here, the tracks headed "cross country" through a somewhat open suburban area without following any railroad tracks or roads. The next stops were at Villa Avenue and Ardmore Avenue in Villa Park. Neither stop had been established when the CA&E began service but were added later, about 1911, as the two towns of Villa Park and Ardmore sprang up. Ardmore was later to become a part of Villa Park.

The first Villa Avenue stations were east of the crossing, but a new station was built in 1929 on the west side of Villa Avenue. It was reportedly the first commercial building in DuPage County to be heated by natural gas. The west half of the building held the CA&E's ticket agent and passenger waiting room. The east half was a store front for the local gas company to display and sell gas-operated appliances. In later years the space was occupied by other businesses including a drug store.

Like the Elmhurst stops at York and Spring Roads, the two Villa Park stops were traditionally served by the local and express trains, but by the 1950's were served by some limiteds. Ardmore Avenue was about 18 miles from Wells Street Terminal in Chicago and required about 37 minutes running time on an express train in the late 1940's.

Leaving Villa Park, CA&E's double track main line entered the Village of Lombard. Lombard was large enough to warrant four stations on the CA&E. The first of these was located at Meyers Road and was called Westmore. This was served by both local and express trains but was bypassed by most limiteds. Westmore, about 19 miles from Wells Street Terminal, had passing sidings in both directions which could be used by either short freight trains or passenger trains. The Westmore stop was relatively new, having been put in during the early 1930's when the population of Lombard reached out to this point.

Above: **Pullman car #403 heads a two-car train at the Westmore Av. station in 1948. The motorman appears to be taking an interest in the photographer on the other side of Meyers Road.** EDWARD FRANK JR. / RICHARD ALLERMANN COLLECTION.

Below: **Pullman car #414 pulls up to the Stewart Ave. stop in April of 1955. Stewart Ave. was earlier known as East Lombard and although it did not warrant a station building, it did have a shelter and a flagstop semaphore.** RICHARD ALLERMANN.

These two photos show westbound trains at Lombard in 1948. Lombard's Main Street is in the foreground.
  Above: **General Electric freight locomotives #2001-2002 head a short freight bound towards Wheaton. Paired freight locomotives were typical on the CA&E.**
  Below: **Niles car #302 heads a three car train of woods on what was probably a Wheaton local.** BOTH PHOTOS EDWARD FRANK JR. / RICHARD ALLERMANN COLLECTION.

Glen Oak was a favorite spot for photographers and fan trip photo stops over the years because of its scenic location. Hicks car #309 heads a two car westbound fan trip stopped at the station while the photographer achieves the vantage point of the Hill Avenue overpass. The short Glen Oak siding can be seen just behind the train. DANIEL E. FRIZANE COLLECTION.

Continuing west, the next stop was at Stewart Avenue in Lombard. Stewart Avenue was a relatively unimportant stop served only by local trains, although it had been in use since 1902 when the AE&C started service.

Next came the important stop at Main Street in Lombard. Located about 20 miles from Wells Street Terminal, this was considered the main stop in Lombard and had been in use since the line was built. During the 1940's, every train stopped here except for the very important limiteds such as the Cannonball. For most limiteds, this was their first scheduled stop beyond Maywood, giving them a non-stop run of 9 miles over good CA&E double track main line. During the late 1940's, a mid-day limited was scheduled to cover the 20 miles in 38 minutes; not a bad showing considering operation over the "L" and several stops.

The fourth and final stop in Lombard was located at Green Valley and was also known as West Lombard. This, just a few blocks from the junction of St. Charles Road and Crescent Blvd., Green Valley was a flag stop and was served by local trains.

West of Green Valley was the most scenic, if not the most costly, segment of CA&E's double track main line. Substantial cut and fill work was used to bridge the Du Page River Valley, and there were no street

---

PRECEDING PAGE

The date was August 16, 1945, when this eastbound two-car train crossed Brewster Street at the Green Valley stop on the west side of Lombard. Pullman car #416 was still wearing its war time "Fly for Navy" livery. MACBEAN / RICHARD ALLERMANN COLLECTION.

---

crossings at grade until Park Boulevard in Glen Ellyn, a distance of about two miles. West of Green Valley, the double track main line began climbing up on a high fill which carried the tracks over Finley Road and then on to a rather modern looking concrete bridge over Illinois Highway 53. Shortly after that the tracks bridged the Du Page river itself.

After crossing the river, the tracks ran through a deep cut and passed the Glen Oak station. The Glen Oak stop was named for the golf course just south of the tracks at this point. In earlier years there was appreciable golf patronage here, but in later years Glen Oak was not particularly important and warranted stops by only the local trains. What it lacked in passengers, however, Glen Oak made up for as a scenic spot to photograph CA&E trains. Trains could be photographed nicely from the sides of the cut or from Hill Avenue which passed overhead. Consequently, this area was a favorite stopping point on fan trips.

Leaving the Glen Oak station, trains would pass under Hill Avenue, the only road bridging over CA&E's double track main line. Leaving the cut, the tracks began climbing again and came up along the south side of the Chicago & North Western's West Line, which they paralleled all the way to Wheaton. Unlike the CGW, the C&NW was a major commuter carrier and was traditionally the biggest competitor to the CA&E. The next stop was at Taylor Avenue, the first of two stops for Glen Ellyn and the least important of the two. Taylor Avenue was traditionally served only by local trains.

Shortly after leaving Taylor Avenue, the CA&E tracks crossed Park Blvd. at grade, the first grade crossing since the Green Valley stop. The main stop for

Above: A westbound fan trip at Glen Oak seen from track level. This time, Cincinnati car #425 is running as a single car. The Hill Street overpass can be seen in the distance. GREG HEIER COLLECTION.

Below: Pullman car #417 heads a four-car train westbound towards Wheaton. The location is between Glen Oak and Taylor Avenue. At this point, the CA&E line emerges from the scenic Glen Oak cut and starts running parallel to the C&NW tracks. GREG HEIER COLLECTION.

Above: **Looking east from the Taylor Ave. station on April 18, 1938. On the left is the main line of the C&NW. In the distance, the CA&E tracks cut away from the steam road for a long stretch through Glen Oak uninterrupted by grade crossings.** JACK BAILEY / SHORE LINE INTERURBAN HISTORICAL SOCIETY.

Below: **The new Glen Ellyn station was designed by John Archibald Armstrong and was erected in 1926. The company was so proud of the new station that it took this photo with some of the new Pullman cars.** LEE HESTERMAN.

Sunset Lines • 67

Above: Discontinuance of passenger service was only a week away when this photo was taken on June 27, 1957. Pullman car #410 leads a St. Louis car on an eastbound run near College Avenue on the east side of Wheaton. The neighboring C&NW tracks are visible to the right. PAUL STRINGHAM / RICHARD ALLERMANN COLLECTION.

Below: In the distance is a westbound train about to round the big curve near College Avenue, Wheaton. The neighboring Chicago & North Western tracks can be seen to the north. T. L. MCCONNELL COLLECTION.

The Wheaton station could occasionally be a busy place for train watchers. Pullman car #412 heads a two-car westbound Wheaton Limited that has just dropped off the last of its passengers at the Wheaton station and is heading for the yard. To the right, a Chicago train is busy loading passengers at the Wheaton station platform. Meanwhile, to the left, a commuter train is making a stop at the adjacent Chicago & North Western station. STEVE MICHAEL COLLECTION.

Glen Ellyn was located on Main Street near the downtown area, as one would expect of any interurban. The original station at Main Street was not much more than a wooden shack. It was later replaced by one of the more attractive stations on the line, following the "cottage" style of architecture common in downtown Glen Ellyn.

In population, Glen Ellyn was the largest community between Lombard and the Fox River, even exceeding Wheaton's population by a small percentage. The CA&E and the C&NW were in a constant battle for passengers between here and Chicago. Main Street in Glen Ellyn was located approximately 23 miles from Wells Street Terminal and usually warranted stops by all trains except the most important limiteds such as the Cannonball. In the late 1940's, limited trains making only one stop west of Maywood (at Lombard) would cover the distance in 43 minutes, an average of over 32 miles per hour including stops.

Continuing west from Glen Ellyn, the CA&E tracks remained adjacent to the C&NW tracks on their south side. Both began a rather gradual and sweeping turn to the south through a relatively open and unpopulated area. CA&E trains, particularly the limiteds, could make up some time here. The next stop was at College Avenue on the west side of Wheaton. The street received its name from famous Wheaton College, located about ½ mile west of the stop and closer to downtown Wheaton. Situated 24 miles from Wells Street, the College Avenue stop was usually served only by local trains. Originally somewhat ignored by the neighboring C&NW, the College Avenue stop assumed greater importance for it after the CA&E had abandoned service.

Chicago Aurora & Elgin trains followed the south side of the C&NW tracks into Wheaton. Passing just to the north of the old County Courthouse, both sets of tracks emerged into downtown Wheaton. The CA&E tracks were hemmed in by Liberty Street on the south and the C&NW tracks on the north as they went through town. Wheaton was both the major junction point for the CA&E as well as the location of its shops and yards.

Sunset Lines • 69

7

Cook County and Westchester Branches

Neither the Cook County nor Westchester branches were significant to CA&E passenger service in its last few years. Passenger service was long gone on the Cook County branch, except for an occasional railfan charter, although much of the branch remained in use for freight service. The Westchester branch had been built by the CA&E but was operated by Chicago's Rapid Transit. It was abandoned in 1951, several years before the CA&E discontinued its own passenger service. The histories of these two branches are somewhat intertwined because of both proximity in location and a relationship in passenger service.

Cook County Branch

The Cook County branch was somewhat unique when compared to the other CA&E branches, as it was operated entirely by overhead trolley wire and was relatively short, approximately 2 miles. Cook County branch trackage left the main line just west of the Bellwood station. Tracks then crossed Mannheim Road just south of the main line. In later years Mannheim became a very busy 4-lane roadway through suburbia. After crossing Mannheim, the branch turned south and was essentially a side-of-the-road operation along the west side of Mannheim. To the west of the tracks was a quarry and some industrial property which later became important for CA&E carload freight. The Indiana Harbor Belt Railroad also had a branch line parallel to the CA&E at this point. In particular, the primary industry at this location was the Consumers Company, which produced aggregates and limestone fertilizers.

The first regular stop on the line south of Bellwood was in the vicinity of Harrison Street. Early records refer to this stop as Jernstrom's Gardens although the exact location of the stop is somewhat unclear. Jernstrom's Gardens was undoubtedly a small, private picnic grove that was popular at this time. It undoubtedly also served as an appropriate spot for refreshments or a reception following a funeral at the nearby cemeteries.

Continuing south, the single track passed under the Illinois Central's main line to Iowa (this was the same track that interchanged with the CA&E at Elgin Junction on the Elgin branch). Beyond the IC was a passing siding and the track began turning west to cross over some marshy ground and a small creek. When the branch was built, the Illinois Central had provided the only public transportation into the area of the cemeteries. However, the AE&C connecting service via Bellwood was soon better patronized than the less-frequent steam road service.

The Cook County branch track then began running west along the north side of Roosevelt Road. A stop and a short passing siding was located north of Oak Ridge Cemetery. Passengers going to Oak Ridge had to cross Roosevelt Road as the cemetery was located on the south side of the road. Continuing west, the single track crossed Wolf Road (then an unimproved dirt road), and terminated on the grounds of the Mt. Carmel Cemetery, approximately 2 miles from the main line. The terminal at Mt. Carmel consisted of two stub-end tracks with a raised platform.

Normal service on the branch was a single car operating as a shuttle from Bellwood to Oak Ridge and Mt. Carmel. At Bellwood, the car left from a short stub track just south of the main line tracks. The car operated from about 9:00 a.m. to about 7:00 p.m., the usual hours one would visit a cemetery. Normal running time from Bellwood to Mt. Carmel was seven minutes. Two round trips were scheduled each hour. The passing sidings were there to permit the regular

---

PRECEDING PAGE

What with trolley wire operation, single track, and shuttle cars in the early days, CA&E's Cook County branch provided a completely different appearance and type of operation than most other CA&E trackage. This view of the branch looks south from Harrison Street in 1932. The Illinois Central overpass is in the distance and Mannheim Road is off to the far left. GEORGE KRAMBLES.

Sunset Lines • 71

Above: Niles car #304 and Jewett car #321 are eastbound at the Bellwood station in 1943. The Bellwood shuttle car started and ended its run on the stub end track on the left. Not far behind the photographer was the point where the Westchester branch cut off to the left. EDWARD FRANK / RICHARD ALLERMANN COLLECTION.

Below: February 12, 1939, saw a fan trip over the Cook County branch using Chicago Rapid Transit cars #4317 and #4401. Here, the fan trip train is on the Cook County branch just south of the Bellwood station. To the left of the train is the IHB freight track and Mannheim Road, and in the distance are the crossing gates for the CA&E mainline and the CGW. GEORGE KRAMBLES.

shuttle car to get around the chartered funeral trains which also used the branch.

Following the opening of the branch in 1906, a single wooden interurban car was normally assigned to the shuttle. Suburban car #30 was borrowed from the North Shore Line and was used on the branch during its final years of operation between 1924 and 1926.

Regular rail passenger service on the Cook County branch ended on October 31, 1926, one month after rapid transit service had started on the Westchester branch. On the following day, the CA&E instituted a replacement bus service. This bus service met rapid transit trains at the new Westchester Terminal at Roosevelt Road (12th Street) and operated to Oak Ridge and Mt. Carmel Cemeteries. After the discontinuance of regular passenger service, much of the Cook County branch was retained for carload freight service, although some chartered funeral cars operated as late as 1934.

In the late 1930's, after rail passenger service had ended on the branch, the passenger platforms were eventually removed as was the track beyond the old Oak Ridge stop. The track along Roosevelt Road to the old Oak Ridge stop fell into disuse but was retained for many years.

Freight service to the monument company, near the point where the tracks reached Roosevelt Road, continued at least into the 1950's and the overhead was maintained to this point.

Because of the quarry sidings and industrial siding, the branch became an important generator of carload freight for the CA&E. Reports indicate that the branch was repaired in the 1950's to facilitate freight operations. From time to time, the branch did see passenger cars as fan trips operated here occasionally.

Some of the trackage was replaced due to expressway construction in the late 1950's. The single track, plus a narrow roadway, were placed on a new bridge over the expressway immediately west of the Mannheim Road interchange. This was used only briefly by the CA&E prior to abandonment.

A portion of the branch was one of the three segments of the CA&E retained for use by other railroads after abandonment, and was the largest surviving segment of CA&E trackage. After CA&E freight service was discontinued in 1959, the Indiana Harbor Belt used some of the CA&E trackage for freight service. Eventually, the CA&E trackage from Mannheim Road south to Oak Ridge was acquired by the IHB. The Illinois Central was also authorized to install a new connecting track to reach and serve the branch from their main line track. The IHB eventually abandoned the CA&E track from Mannheim to Harrison and south of the IC overpass. The remaining CA&E track was taken out of service in 1986.

Westchester Branch

The Westchester branch was built by the Chicago Westchester & Western Railroad, a subsidiary which was incorporated into the CA&E in 1926. What makes the Westchester branch so unusual is that although it was built and owned by the CA&E, it was operated by Chicago Rapid Transit under a contract executed on July 31, 1925. In contrast to the Cook County branch, the Westchester branch was equipped entirely with third rail.

The Westchester branch was originally planned under the Conway organization. Recent research suggests that the Conway staff was far along in planning a high-speed bypass route via the Westchester branch, Cermak Road, and Butterfield Road to connect with

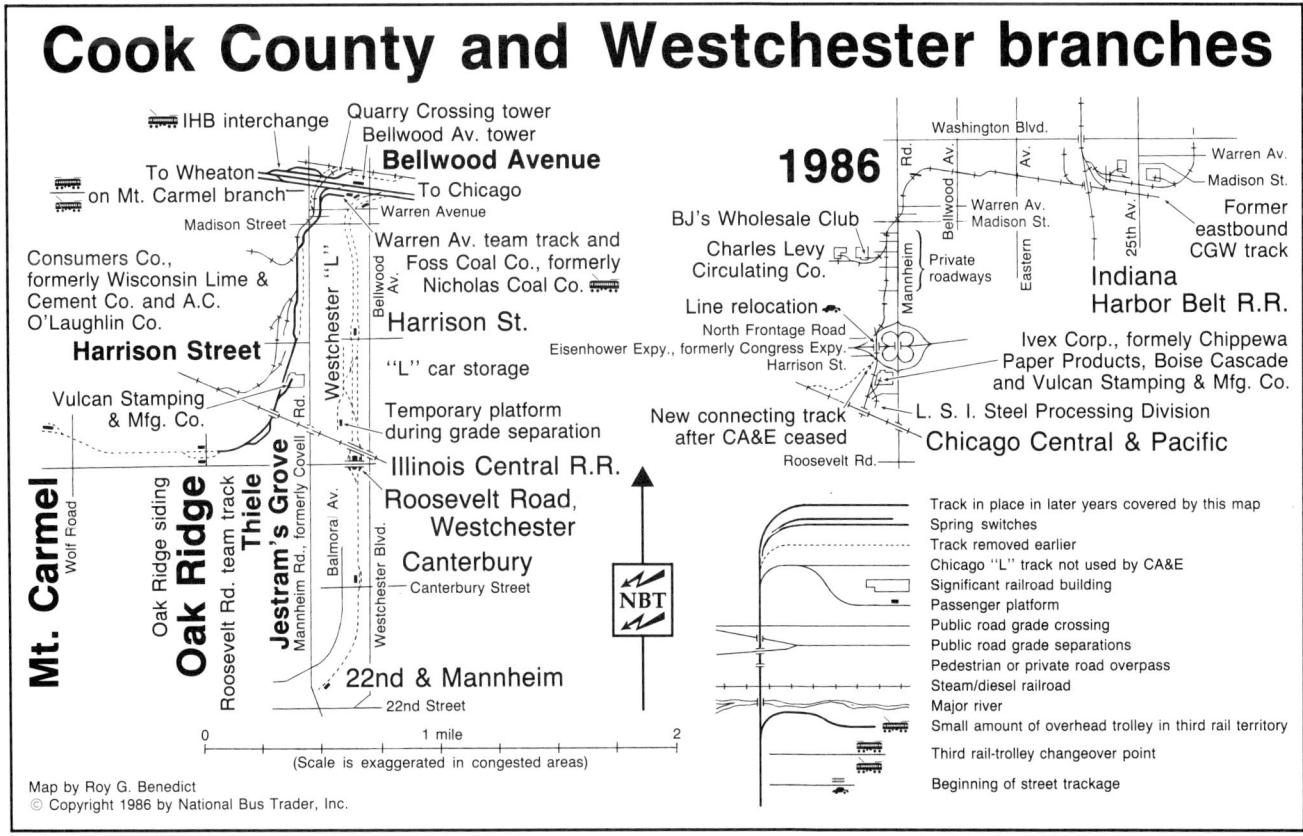

Above: July 3, 1949, found Hicks car #310 and Jewett car #318 being used for the ERA Convention Special train. This photo was taken at Madison Street, near where the branch crossed Mannheim Road. It is interesting that the date of this trip and photo was exactly eight years before all CA&E passenger service was discontinued. EDWARD FRANK JR. / RICHARD ALLERMANN COLLECTION.

Below: Here is another view of the 1939 Chicago Rapid Transit private excursion over the Cook County-Mt. Carmel branch. This photo was taken near Harrison Street. EDWARD FRANK JR. / RICHARD ALLERMANN COLLECTION.

Above: **St. Louis car #459 approached the IC overpass while on a fan trip. The siding to the right served the Vulcan Stamping & Mfg. Co. Some trackage in this area was switched by the Indiana Harbor Belt until 1986.** DANIEL E. FRIZANE COLLECTION

Below: **Hicks car #310 went over the Cook County-Mt. Carmel branch on a fan trip run on August 8, 1954. The location is adjacent to the Illinois Central overpass.** ROBERT A. SELLE / RICHARD ALLERMANN COLLECTION.

Above: Yet another view of the February 12, 1939, excursion over the Cook County branch using Chicago Rapid Transit #4317 and #4401. The two cars are on the east side of Mannheim Road, immediately south of the Bellwood station and CA&E mainline. The IHB freight track is in the foreground. GEORGE KRAMBLES.

Below: Freight service rather than passenger equipment was more typical on the Cook County branch after 1934. Here locomotives #2001-2002 switch some older box cars near the IC overpass. The date was April 12, 1959; passenger service had already ended and the freight locomotives were running their last miles. LARRY KOSTKA.

Just east of CA&E's Bellwood station the Westchester branch cut off to the south. Cincinnati car #430 is on the back of a two-car CA&E train on the main line headed east. The Westchester line tracks can be seen branching to the right at the bottom of the photo. GREG HEIER COLLECTION.

the Aurora branch and hence bypass the western suburbs. This may well explain why the Westchester branch was built into an area which appeared to be too lightly populated to support rapid transit service.

In design, the Westchester branch was of rapid transit quality with high level platforms and third rail. Double track extended south to Roosevelt Road with single track beyond. The track was at grade for much of the distance and had at least four street crossings. The branch was to the east of Mannheim Road and only a short walk east of the Cook County branch.

The Westchester branch diverged from the CA&E main line with a double track interlocked junction just east of the Bellwood station. The two tracks made a sweeping turn to the south through the rapid transit Bellwood station, which was separate from the CA&E Bellwood station. From here, the double track continued south to the next station at Harrison Street. This consisted of a center island high level platform.

Continuing south from Harrison, the line remained double track with the addition of car storage tracks on the west. The Westchester branch double track passed under both the IC track and Roosevelt Road. The station at Roosevelt Road was an island platform in between the two tracks.

Roosevelt Road was the end of the line from 1926 until 1930, when an extension was built south to Cermak Road. Testimony before the Illinois Commerce Commission indicated that the track was initially halted at Roosevelt Road when the Department of Public Works and Buildings, Division of State Highways, refused permission for a crossing of Roosevelt Road at grade. Subsequently, the State approved a grade separated crossing with the rail line passing below Roosevelt Road. On November 13, 1929,

the Illinois Commerce Commission approved the 4,500-foot extension south from Roosevelt Road by the Chicago Aurora & Elgin, which by that time had absorbed the Chicago Westchester & Western.

Immediately south of Roosevelt Road, the two tracks combined into a single track going south. A stop with a high level platform was located at Canterbury Street. Continuing south, the single track began a sweeping turn to the west. A platform and station building were located at the end of track for Cermak Road (22nd Street). If the bypass route had been built, the track would have been continued under Mannheim Road and along the north side of Cermak Road. Normal service saw the regular rapid transit trains operate to the Roosevelt Road station and turn there. A rapid transit shuttle train normally served the single track section between Roosevelt and Cermak.

Chicago Rapid Transit started service on the Westchester branch on October 1, 1926. The rapid transit extended its service from Forest Park over the CA&E main line to Bellwood and then south to Roosevelt Road on the branch. At this time the rapid transit also took over local service between Chicago and Bellwood. Roosevelt Road remained the south terminal for the Westchester branch until December of 1930, when service was extended south to Cermak Road.

The Chicago Transit Authority discontinued rail service to Westchester on December 9, 1951. Forest Park once again became the western terminal for rapid transit service. At this time the CTA replaced Westchester rail service with a bus route which connected with rapid transit trains at Forest Park. The Westchester branch had never been used for freight service and was dismantled after CTA passenger service was discontinued.

Sunset Lines • 77

Above: A single-car Chicago Rapid Transit train is headed south, approaching the Roosevelt Road stop. The rapid transit storage track can be seen to the west. An obvious lack of homes in the area was reflected in the line's patronage. SHORE LINE INTERURBAN HISTORICAL SOCIETY.

Below: Chicago Rapid Transit car #2806 heads a train pausing at the Roosevelt Road stop. Roosevelt Road itself crosses overhead. From here, the train will head north to Bellwood and then east to Chicago's Loop. GREG HEIER COLLECTION.

Above: Chicago Rapid Transit steel "L" car #4395 on the Westchester branch in 1937. The location is the southern terminal at Mannheim & 22nd Street and we suspect that the flag may indicate a holiday. Normal service to this point on the line was run by a single car shuttle from Roosevelt Road. EDWARD FRANK JR. / RICHARD ALLERMANN COLLECTION.

Below: The only stop on the Westchester branch between Roosevelt road and the end-of-line at 22nd street was at Canterbury St. A steel Chicago Rapid Transit car crosses Canterbury Street on November 20, 1941, only days before the United States entered World War II. The trolley poles were superfluous on Westchester cars since the entire line from Chicago's loop to 22nd & Mannheim was third-rail equipped. CHARLES A. BROWN / SHORE LINE INTERURBAN HISTORICAL SOCIETY.

8

Wheaton

During the life of the Chicago Aurora & Elgin, Wheaton was an important and interesting place. It was the major junction point for the railroad, the location of the shops and most car storage, and the location for operating management. Although the seat of Du Page County, Wheaton's population in the late 1930's was still less than 10,000.

The Chicago Aurora & Elgin tracks approached Wheaton from the east by paralleling the south side of the Chicago & North Western tracks. CA&E's tracks passed just north of the old County Courthouse, and then entered downtown Wheaton by running in a relatively narrow strip which was south of the Chicago & North Western tracks and on the north edge of Liberty Street. The Wheaton Station was located approximately 25 miles from Chicago's Loop. The fastest CA&E trains would make the trip from Wells Street to Wheaton in only 40 minutes while locals required closer to an hour.

Wheaton was always the scene of much switching activity. Local and express trains to Wheaton would discharge their last passengers at the Wheaton Station and then continue about three blocks west to the yard. At least in the later years, the limited trains would normally carry through cars to both Aurora and Elgin on either end of the train with one or more Wheaton cars in the center. This procedure permitted adding a Wheaton car to either the Aurora or Elgin through cars if ridership beyond Wheaton warranted. Normally, two breaks were made in limited trains to separate them into Aurora, Wheaton, and Elgin trains or cars. A single car was typical for mid-day service on the branches.

In addition to the breaking of trains, there was also the activity of additional motormen "making up their cab" in the cars being cut. A similar but reverse procedure was followed on eastbound limited trains.

Prior to 1953, eastbound and westbound limited trains tended to meet at or near the Wheaton Station hourly at about five minutes before the hour. This permitted the branch line cars to reach Aurora and Elgin, spend ten minutes changing ends, and return to Wheaton in time to meet the next eastbound limited from Chicago. Hence, the schedule called for only one train at a time on each branch and eliminated a need for meets in single track territory. After 1953, most mid-day limited trains still met in the vicinity of the Wheaton Station but they now operated 90 minutes apart, and enjoyed almost 40 minutes to change ends at Aurora and Elgin.

Westbound from the Wheaton Station, the double track main line continued between Liberty Street and the Chicago & North Western tracks for about three blocks before entering the CA&E yard property. Just before entering the yard, you could glance south across Liberty Street and see the modern building at 400 W. Liberty which was built in the late 1940's and served as General Offices for the interurban in its later years.

The old interlocking tower, which also served as a dispatcher's office, was placed in service in October of 1906 and was located in the "wye" formed by the divergence of the Aurora and Elgin branches. From this vantage point, someone in the tower could see arriving trains from any of the three directions. In the 1940's, a new brick tower was constructed slightly northeast of the old one, on the north side of the double track line from the Wheaton station.

PRECEDING PAGE

This unusual view was photographed from the northeast corner of Wheaton yards and looks east into Wheaton. The C&NW tracks are on the far left (north). Next are the CA&E tracks heading east to the Wheaton station and beyond to Chicago. South of the CA&E tracks is Liberty Drive, which paralleled the interurban tracks through downtown Wheaton. In the distance is the tower of the Du Page County Courthouse. On the far right is the building at 400 W. Liberty which housed the CA&E offices in the later years. Cincinnati car #426 appears to be inbound from Elgin and about to cross Liberty Drive, heading east and away from the camera. The car will run on the westbound main track for a few more feet until it reaches the crossover to get on the eastbound track. Another car is visible in the distance near the CA&E station; perhaps the car from Aurora has already arrived and is awaiting the Elgin car to come up behind and couple.

JAMES BARRICK / RICHARD ALLERMANN COLLECTION.

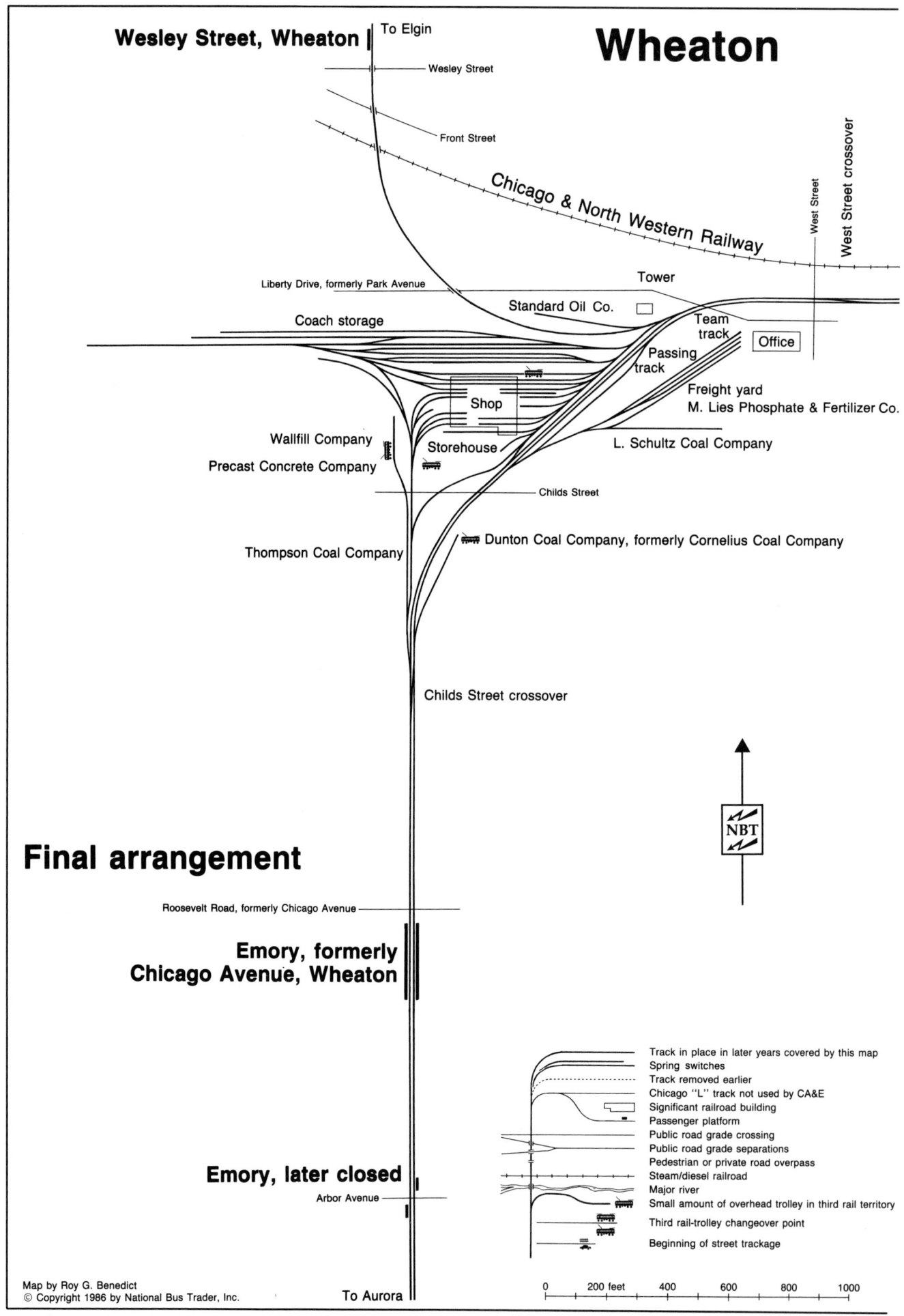

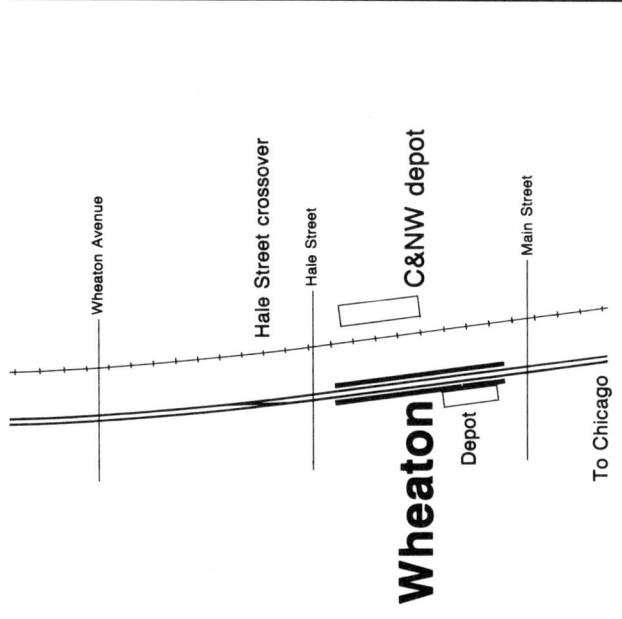

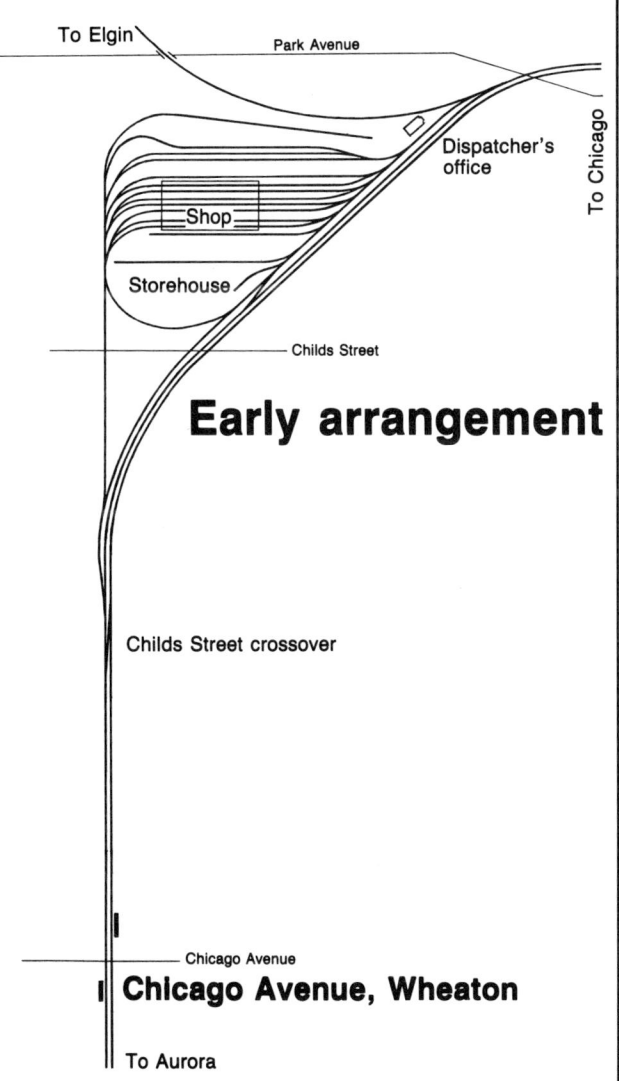

Early arrangement

Chicago Avenue, Wheaton

The double track main line turned southwest through the Wheaton yard and headed towards Aurora. The single track Elgin branch diverged from the westbound main and made a climbing curve to the north to cross the Chicago & North Western tracks on a bridge. The main shop and yard lead track diverged from the Elgin track within feet of the main line. This, like the twin tracks headed towards Aurora, curved in a southwesterly direction.

The north end of the property was taken up by several (the number varies through the years) rather long yard tracks used for car storage. South of this was the shop complex. In order to get operations started quickly, the AE&C erected a temporary shop building on the site in May of 1902. This original building was of frame construction and was 30 feet by 80 feet in size. By October of 1902, masons were busy laying brick for the permanent machine and repair shop at Wheaton. This measured 200 feet square and survived until the end of operations. The older and temporary frame shops building was torn down soon after the permanent building was completed. The Conway organization added a carpentry and paint shop to the earlier building in 1922, making the entire structure quite large and elaborate. Some of the track in the yard, particularly that near the shop complex, was powered by trolley wire rather than third rail.

Because of limited storage facilities elsewhere on the line, most passenger and all freight and work equipment was kept at Wheaton when not operating on the line. Consequently, other than during weekday rush hours, there was always a wide range of equipment to be seen and photographed at Wheaton.

This two-car train has paused at the Wheaton station to receive and discharge passengers. It will soon continue east to Chicago and away from the camera. Cincinnati car #433 brings up the rear of the train while one of the St. Louis cars appears to be on the head end. Normal CA&E procedure called for the making and breaking of limited trains here at the Wheaton station platform. Cars to and from the branches would operate individually from here to the yard or the junction switch, often only a few car-lengths apart. In later years, the head car on a westbound limited would normally continue on to Aurora. Occasionally, extra cars to Wheaton only would separate the through Aurora car from the through Elgin car. DANIEL E. FRIZANE.

Sunset Lines • 83

Above: **The new Wheaton station was constructed in 1911 and was somewhat modified in later years. At all times during the history of the CA&E it was a busy location and a major junction point. Here Pullman car #416 heads an eastbound train to Chicago while St. Louis #451 brings up the rear on a westbound train. Limited trains meeting at or near Wheaton was typical of schedules in later years.** DANIEL E. FRIZANE COLLECTION.

Below: **This photo of the Wheaton station looks east and was taken from Hale Street, the next crossing west of the station building. It appears that once again the eastbound and westbound limiteds have met at the Wheaton station. Immediately adjacent on the left is the station of the competition, the Chicago & North Western.** GREG HEIER COLLECTION.

84 • *Sunset Lines*

Above: St. Louis car #460 operates west from the Wheaton station towards the yard and junction. Liberty Drive is on the left while the C&NW tracks are on the far right. It looks like the westbound limited has just been cut at Wheaton, as you can see another car about two blocks ahead of #460. One or both cars will probably head up the branches to continue their runs to Aurora or Elgin. DANIEL E. FRIZANE COLLECTION.

Below: This view looks southwesterly in front of the shops. On the left are the two tracks leading to Aurora. Pullman car #409 and one of the freight locomotives are parked in front of the shop. TIMOTHY C. IVERSON COLLECTION.

Above: This interior view of the old shop building shows some of the machinery, equipment, and shop personnel needed to keep the interurbans running. Cincinnati car #427 is on the far right. DANIEL E. FRIZANE COLLECTION.

Below: This view shows the interior of the newer carpentry and paint shop. Car #436, on the right, was somewhat unique as it was rebuilt from old parlor car #600 in 1929. The pile on the left appears to include some seat parts. DANIEL E. FRIZANE COLLECTION.

Above: **The Wheaton yard was also home base for the CA&E freight and work equipment as well as the passenger cars. Here, locomotives #2001-2002 sit in front of the shop between freight runs. The sign on the building leaves no doubt as to the location.** GREG HEIER.

Below: **The back of the shop was not quite as presentable, but could often be more interesting. Most of the yards tracks were powered by third rail, but some tracks close to the shop were powered by trolley wire as a safety consideration for employees.** DANIEL E. FRIZANE.

Sunset Lines • 87

Above: The storage tracks on the north side of the yard extended a considerable distance to the west. A walk to the end of track produced this view of stately Niles car #301. The shop building would be in the distance and off to the right. LARRY PLACHNO COLLECTION.

Below: The Wheaton yard was also home base for the work equipment. Car #7 had originally been used as an express car but by this time had been designated as a tool car. Note that the car carried conventional couplers so that it could haul conventional railroad cars. DANIEL E. FRIZANE.

Above: Since the Wheaton yard provided almost the only car storage area on the CA&E, the saying "as lonely as Wheaton yard in the rush hour" became popular among Midwest traction people. Obviously the opposite must also be true, and is proven by this photo. A Sunday morning in July of 1942 provided the photographer this delightful scene including #435, #201, #307, and #319 on the storage tracks north of the shop. VICTOR G. WAGNER.

Below: The Standard Oil siding on the far north of the yard was often also used for car storage. A string of ex-North Shore cars rests in that location in this photo. The track to the left going up the embankment is the Elgin branch. GREG HEIER COLLECTION.

9

Aurora Branch

The Aurora line always had a special position with the Chicago Aurora & Elgin. Construction of the railroad had actually started in Aurora in 1900 and then proceeded to Wheaton and Chicago. When scheduled service started in 1902, it initially operated from Laramie Avenue to Aurora. Hence, the first trackage to be built by the AE&C was in Aurora and it remained in service until the very end. Technically, the line from Aurora to Wheaton was not a branch in the real meaning of the word. As late as the 1940's, various official documents spoke of a "main line" from Aurora to Chicago with branches to Batavia and Elgin. And consequently, the Aurora line was more properly considered the main line of the railroad. It might also be remembered that the original name of the railroad used its home office city, Aurora, first to show that community's importance.

In basic design, the Aurora branch was a single track line with third rail power extending from Wheaton to Aurora. Unlike the Elgin branch, the Aurora branch had three substantial sections of double track, each equipped with spring switches, which could be used for meets. In addition, the Batavia branch diverged from the Aurora branch at Batavia (Eola) Junction and ran to the community of Batavia on the Fox River.

Aurora trains left Wheaton westbound on the double track main line between Liberty Street and the Chicago & North Western tracks. About three blocks later the main line entered the CA&E's Wheaton yard property. Almost immediately, the Elgin branch and yard lead track diverged from the westbound main. However, both main tracks turned southwest at the start of the Aurora branch. This double track main line continued through the yard with the shop buildings on the west and the freight tracks on the east. At the south end of the CA&E yard the two tracks turned directly south.

The first stop on the branch was at Roosevelt Road, which was earlier known as the Chicago Avenue stop. Slightly further south was a small stop known as Emory. In the mid-1940's the old Emory stop was eliminated and the Chicago Avenue stop became known as Emory. It warranted a tiny little structure that could be considered a station only by the very generous.

South of here the double track line turned to the southwest, crossing Spring Creek, and then came to the Chicago Golf stop. This stop was named because it was located immediately adjacent to the Chicago Golf Club. In the earlier years there was substantial golf traffic on the line and there are indications that some of the parlor car service was geared to these golf patrons.

Continuing southwest, the two tracks merged into one with a spring switch, which started the first single track signal block beyond Wheaton. Much of the Aurora branch single track was built off-center so as to permit installation of a second track at a later date, but the second track was never installed.

Shortly after this the single track reached the Plamondon stop. This was located only 1.7 miles from the Wheaton station. Running time from Wheaton was normally only three or four minutes but some trains received extra time to hold them on double track for a meet. The relatively short double track section from Wheaton to Plamondon served as a long passing siding and gave the Aurora branch some interesting scheduling advantages. Unlike the Elgin branch, it was possible to advance a westbound passenger train or equipment move out of Wheaton several minutes before an eastbound train was due to arrive.

Continuing southwest, the next stop on the CA&E track was at Weisbrook Road, usually two minutes running time from Plamondon. From late 1931 until 1946, there was a small siding located just east of Weisbrook Road. Know as McCormick Siding, it apparently was little used and only had capacity for four cars. The Weisbrook Road stop was established in 1902 when service began and it remained in use until the end of passenger service.

PRECEDING PAGE

At the north end of Aurora, the CA&E tracks turned away from the Fox River and started heading northeast towards Batavia Junction and Wheaton. On a run from Aurora to Chicago, St. Louis car #458 has just left the Aurora Avenue stop and is on the CB&Q crossing while approaching Highway 25. The Fox River can be seen in the background. DANIEL E. FRIZANE COLLECTION.

Sunset Lines • 91

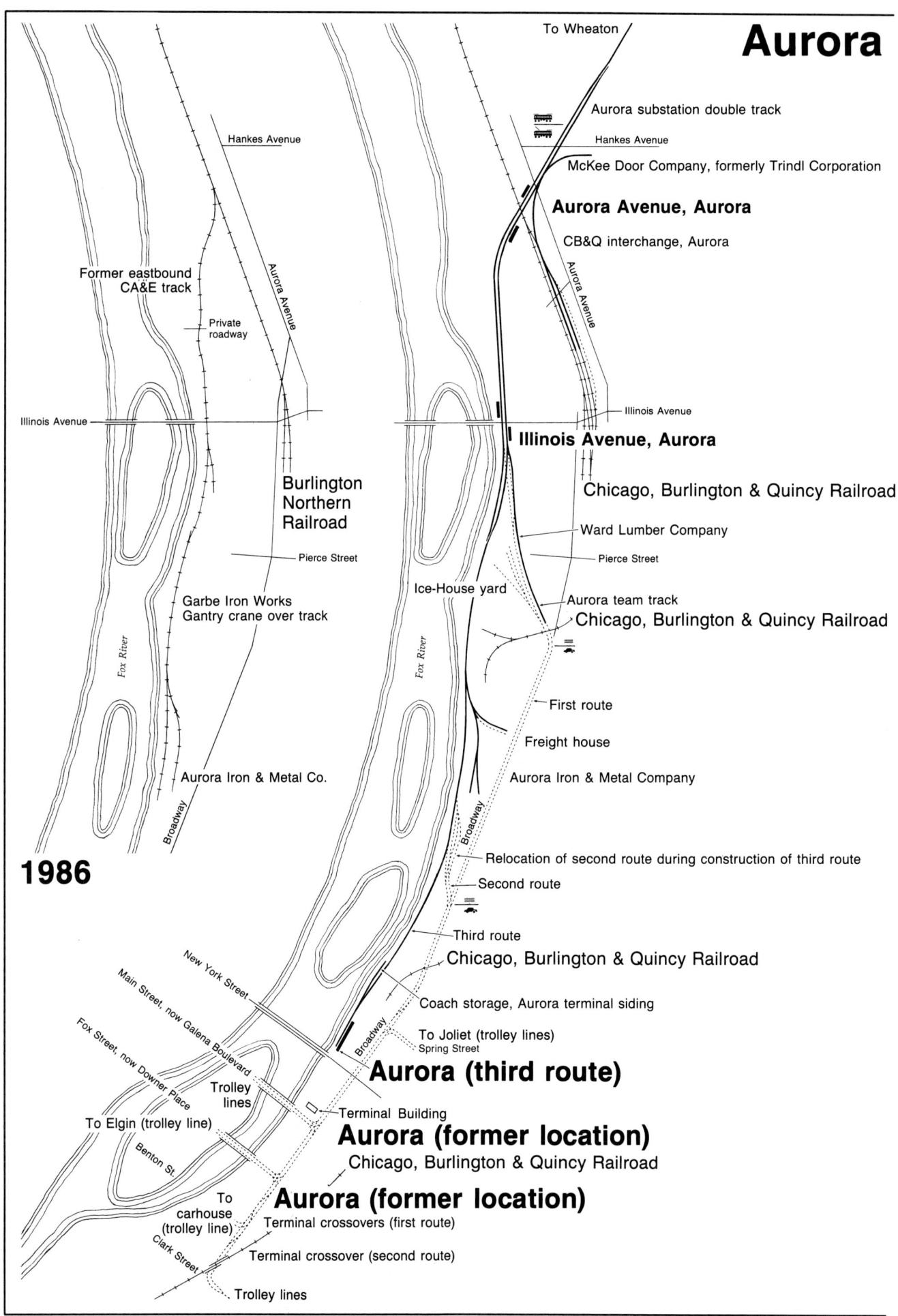

branch

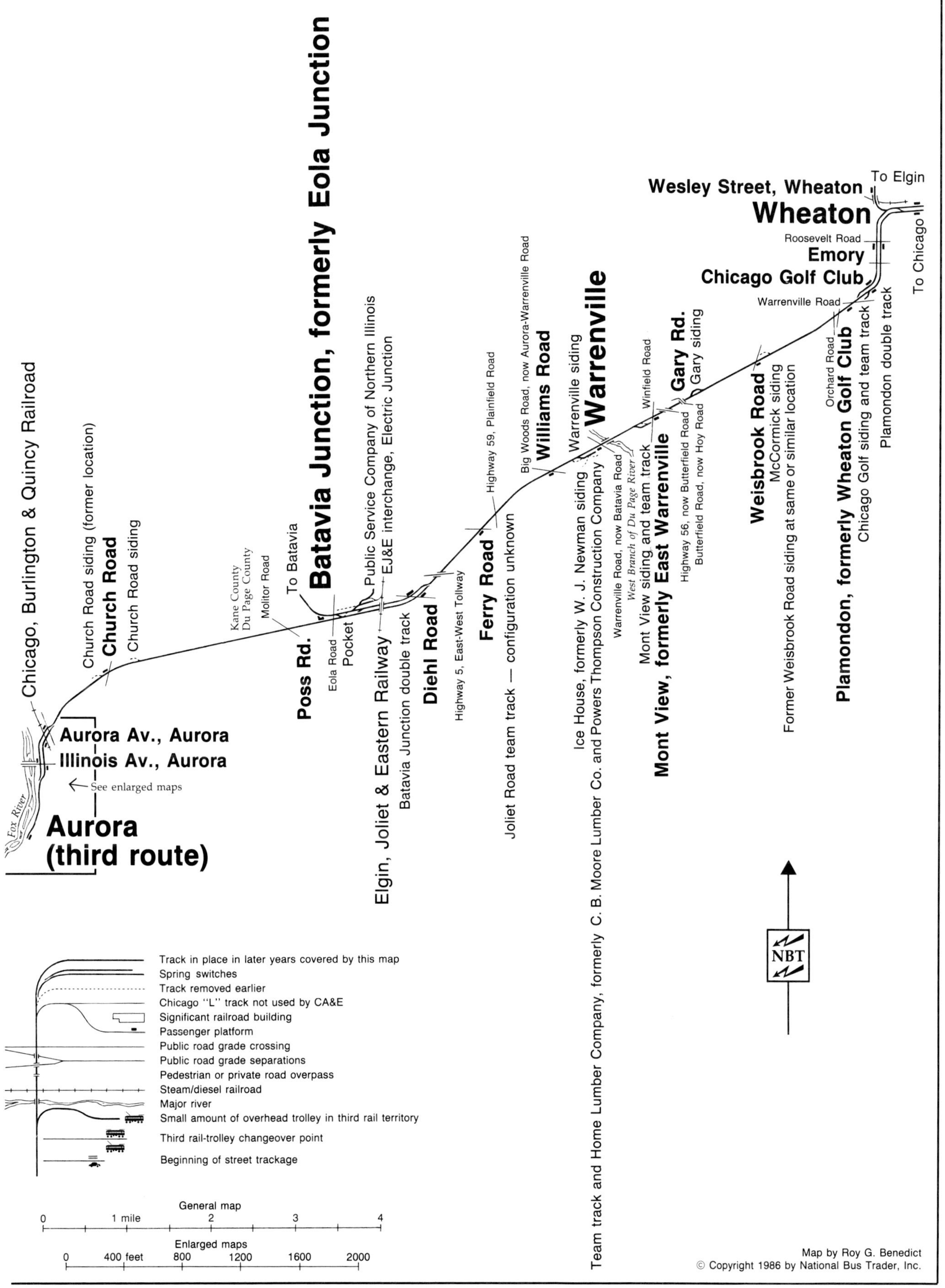

Aurora (third route)

- Chicago, Burlington & Quincy Railroad
- Church Road siding (former location)
- **Church Road**
- Church Road siding
- Aurora Av., Aurora
- Illinois Av., Aurora
- ← See enlarged maps
- Fox River

Poss Rd.
- Kane County / Du Page County
- Molitor Road
- To Batavia
- Eola Road Pocket

Batavia Junction, formerly Eola Junction
- Public Service Company of Northern Illinois
- EJ&E interchange, Electric Junction
- Elgin, Joliet & Eastern Railway
- Batavia Junction double track

Diehl Road
- Highway 5, East-West Tollway

Ferry Road
- Highway 59, Plainfield Road
- Joliet Road team track — configuration unknown
- Big Woods Road, now Aurora-Warrenville Road

Williams Road
- Warrenville siding

Warrenville
- Warrenville Road, now Batavia Road
- West Branch of Du Page River
- Ice House, formerly W. J. Newman siding
- Mont View siding and team track
- Winfield Road

Mont View, formerly East Warrenville
- Highway 56, now Butterfield Road
- Butterfield Road, now Hoy Road

Gary Rd.
- Gary siding

Weisbrook Road
- McCormick siding
- Former Weisbrook Road siding at same or similar location

Plamondon, formerly Wheaton Golf Club
- Chicago Golf Club siding and team track
- Plamondon double track
- Orchard Road

Chicago Golf Club
- **Emory**
- Warrenville Road
- Roosevelt Road

Wheaton
- Wesley Street, Wheaton
- To Elgin
- To Chicago

Team track and Home Lumber Company, formerly C. B. Moore Lumber Co. and Powers Thompson Construction Company

↑ NBT

Legend:
- Track in place in later years covered by this map
- Spring switches
- Track removed earlier
- Chicago "L" track not used by CA&E
- Significant railroad building
- Passenger platform
- Public road grade crossing
- Public road grade separations
- Pedestrian or private road overpass
- Steam/diesel railroad
- Major river
- Small amount of overhead trolley in third rail territory
- Third rail-trolley changeover point
- Beginning of street trackage

General map: 0, 1 mile, 2, 3, 4
Enlarged maps: 0, 400 feet, 800, 1200, 1600, 2000

Map by Roy G. Benedict
© Copyright 1986 by National Bus Trader, Inc.

Above: Many people did not consider the Aurora line a branch, but rather part of the main line. The trackage certainly gave this impression since the double track main line from Chicago continued intact through the Wheaton yard and then out towards Aurora. Here, locomotives #4005-4006 cross Childs Street on the south side of the Wheaton yard. To the left, the two tracks go through the yard and on to Chicago, while on the right they head toward Aurora. GREG HEIER.

Below: The Emory stop was located adjacent to Roosevelt Road, just south of the yard on the south side of Wheaton. It was the first stop on the Aurora branch beyond the main Wheaton station and warranted only passenger platforms and a tiny building. In October of 1951, a two-car train, headed by St. Louis car #453, pounds past Emory in October of 1951. Deep shadows and the two-car train lead one to believe that this may have been the Cannonball. ROBERT W. GIBSON / LARRY KOSTKA COLLECTION.

Above: This official photo from the CA&E file shows the Chicago Golf station in the 1920's. Double track extended from Chicago to a point slightly southwest of here. In the early days, this stop enjoyed substantial patronage from the golfers. JACK R. BAILEY / SHORE LINE INTERURBAN HISTORICAL SOCIETY.

Below: Ex-North Shore cars #134 and #137 were photographed while being used on a fan trip, probably on August 31, 1942. The train was located between Chicago Golf and Plamondon, near where the double track combined into a single track. DANIEL E. FRIZANE COLLECTION.

Above: **This post-abandonment photo shows the end of double track near Plamondon. The track continuing ahead was the eastbound track to Wheaton while the track at the left was the westbound track from Wheaton. This switch was normally spring operated.** GREG HEIER.

Below: **Beyond Plamondon the Aurora branch went down to a single track. Here car #421 heads westbound near Plamondon and the end of double track.** W. C. JANSSEN.

Car #433 is westbound to Aurora on June 27, 1957. The car is crossing Weisbrook Road after dropping off a passenger at the Weisbrook stop. Although neither the motorman nor photographer knew it at the time, passenger service would end in a week. PAUL STRINGHAM / RICHARD ALLERMANN COLLECTION.

If the proposed bypass route had been built in the 1920's or 1930's by the Conway administration, it would have joined the Aurora branch near Weisbrook Road.

Leaving Weisbrook Road, the CA&E track passed just south of a wooded area. Gary siding was located at this point, north of the single track main line, but there was no established stop here. The siding was double-ended but used regular switches and only had a capacity of eight cars. Hence, it was used very little by passenger trains. Gary siding was the end of the first signal block which had started at Plamondon.

Beyond Gary siding the track passed under Butterfield Road and reached a station located at the Winfield Road crossing. Earlier schedules showed this as the East Warrenville stop, but by the early 1940's the name had been changed to Mont View.

Continuing southwest from the Mont View stop, the CA&E track crossed Winfield Road, passed the short (4 car) Mont View siding, and cut through a small corner of a forest preserve. Soon the track crossed the West Branch of the Du Page River, crossed the parallel Batavia Road at grade, and reached Warrenville Station. Located 5.1 miles from Wheaton, most trains required 9 or 10 minutes running time. The Warrenville station was a substantial brick building, possibly because Warrenville was also the location of a manual substation. A canopy covered the platform between the building and train. Warrenville was the only community between Wheaton and Aurora with a recorded population. It was credited with a population of 445 individuals in the 1930 census. The stop was established when the line was built and remained an important stop until passenger service was discontinued.

All trains on the Aurora branch stopped at Warrenville. The exceptions were the evening "Cannonball" and the morning express from Batavia, both prior to 1953's cutback in service to Forest Park.

Immediately west of the Warrenville Station was the Warrenville siding with a capacity of 30 cars. This also marked the end of the second signal block past Plamondon. The Williams Road crossing and stop came next, only one minute southwest of Warrenville.

Beyond Williams Road, the single track continued southwest, crossing Ferry Creek and Illinois Highway 59. Early records indicate the location of Joliet Road Siding at or near Hwy. 59. The siding had a capacity of only four cars and apparently was little used, and hence was taken up at an early date. The next stop was at Ferry Road, scheduled for two minutes from Warrenville. Just beyond Ferry Road was the future site of the new East-West Tollway. When constructed in 1958, the roadway was built above the track to allow freight operations and would have permitted continued passenger operation on the CA&E at this point.

Continuing southwest, the single track encountered a spring switch and became double track. This was the second double track section on the Aurora branch and probably its most important passing point. The third block signal section ended here at the east end of double track. The double track line then crossed Diehl Road where a stop of the same name was located. This stop occurred just before the track crossed the road. Earlier schedules show Diehl Road as a regular stop, but by the mid-1940's only about four trains in each direction stopped here. After the demise of the CA&E, the new Country Lakes Golf Club was built adjacent to this point.

Sunset Lines • 97

Above: This post-abandonment photo was taken from Winfield Road looking east. Immediately across Winfield Road and on the right is the remains of the Mont View stop. In the distance is the Highway 55 (now Illinois route 56) overpass and beyond that is the Butterfield Road overpass. GREG HEIER.

Below: On March 14, 1957, Pullman car #416 operates as a one-car train to Chicago. The location was near the Mont View station and siding. PAUL STRINGHAM / RICHARD ALLERMANN COLLECTION.

Above: St. Louis car #451 was still new when it headed a two-car eastbound Chicago Limited on September 9, 1946. In true interurban tradition, the motorman leans out to watch his passengers load at the Warrenville Station. This station was somewhat unusual by CA&E standards in having a canopy to shelter passengers. VICTOR G. WAGNER.

Below: Warrenville was the only community between Wheaton and Aurora with a significant population. Hicks wood car #309 poses for the railfans on a two-car excursion trip. The photographer, facing northeast, is standing across the tracks from the station shown in the above photo. DANIEL E. FRIZANE.

Above: St. Louis car #457 is westbound to Aurora, approaching Diehl Road. From this point to the EJ&E interchange, the Aurora branch opened up once more to two tracks. Both the switch behind the car and the one at the EJ&E interchange were equipped with springs, making this double track section a long passing siding. W. C. JANSSEN.

Below: Sunday morning August 8, 1954, found Pullman car #406 running a fan trip on the Aurora branch. The car is westbound on the double track section opposite the EJ&E interchange. On the left are the EJ&E interchange tracks while in the distance is the EJ&E overpass. R. SELLE / RICHARD ALLERMANN COLLECTION.

Batavia Junction was the meeting point between Aurora trains and the Batavia branch shuttle cars. It warranted a high level platform but was in a somewhat isolated location. St. Louis car #458 is arriving from Aurora on the left while Cincinnati car #430 is working the Batavia branch, which curves off to the right. STEVE MAGUIRE / RICHARD ALLERMANN COLLECTION

The CA&E double track continued southwest and then passed under the Elgin Joliet & Eastern's outer belt freight line around Chicago. After emerging from under the EJ&E line, the CA&E-EJ&E interchange could be seen to the north. This was a rather elaborate interchange for the CA&E since it included both a receiving and release track with a total capacity of 49 cars.

Opposite the interchange was a crossover with a spring switch which permitted Aurora-bound cars to get back on the south track. If a car was to continue on to Batavia, the car would have to stop, the crew would throw the spring switch to permit passage straight ahead, and then the car would continue west. This ended the double track section which had started just prior to Diehl Road and was used for many Aurora branch meets until the end of passenger service. This also started a new block signal section for trains continuing to Aurora. Although both tracks continued into Batavia Junction, they split at that point with the north track going to Batavia and the south track going to Aurora.

The Batavia Junction station was reached shortly after crossing Eola Road. Originally this stop was named Eola Junction, either because of the nearby road or because the town of Eola is located about 1½ miles south of this point. The old AE&C changed the name to Batavia Junction sometime between 1909 and 1914. The station itself had a high level platform in later years to facilitate the transfer of passengers between Aurora and Batavia cars. This made the station look somewhat incongruous since it was located in the middle of farmland and substantially removed from any appreciable habitation. Since most Batavia service operated as a shuttle between this point and Batavia, the high level platform was a definite asset in speeding up passenger transfers. Batavia Junction was located 8.9 miles from Wheaton and most trains were scheduled to cover this distance in about 15 minutes. All CA&E passenger trains coming past this location made a station stop here.

Beyond Batavia Junction the Aurora branch continued as a single track with third rail power. Heading southwest, the track passed though a rural area with little population. Molitor Road was crossed at grade and then the track left Du Page County to enter Kane County. A bridge carried the track across Indian Creek and the next passenger stop was at Church Road. Passenger facilities at this remote location were minimal and consisted of a tiny shelter and a bench. This was about 3 miles beyond Batavia Junction and most trains were scheduled for only 3 minutes, reflecting the fast running between these two points.

From here the track made a sweeping turn toward the south and entered the outskirts of Aurora. Just before crossing Illinois Highway 25, the single track once more expanded into two tracks with a spring switch and a transition was made from third rail to overhead trolley power. The start of double track ended the block signal section which had started at Batavia Junction. The Aurora substation was located on Hankes Avenue to the south of the tracks. The Aurora Avenue stop was located just beyond this, immediately after crossing Highway 25. Most trains were given only two minutes to reach Aurora Avenue from Church Road. The CB&Q line crossed the CA&E at Aurora Avenue and the interchange was located just to the south of this point.

Above: The long haul from Batavia Junction to the north side of Aurora was substantially devoid of both population and regular stops. In later years, the only regular stop in this area was here at Church Road. The accommodations at this location give you some hint of the small volume of passengers boarding here. GREG HEIER / RICHARD ALLERMANN COLLECTION.

Below: On the north side of Aurora near the Aurora substation, the single track once more split into a double track line by means of a spring switch. This effectively provided a passing siding along the Fox River to a point south of Illinois Avenue. Ex-WB&A car #702, with a two-car fan trip, meets the regular car coming out of Aurora. GREG HEIER COLLECTION.

Above: On August 21, 1955, St. Louis car #451 was inbound to Aurora. It had already changed to the overhead trolley wire and was crossing Highway 25 and rolling into the Aurora Avenue stop. Meanwhile, locomotives #4005–4006 were busy hauling freight out of the neighboring CB&Q interchange. W. D. MIDDLETON / RICHARD ALLERMANN COLLECTION.

Below: Niles car #20 is heading to Aurora on the double track section just south of the Aurora Avenue stop. Although not obvious in this view, the Fox River is just to the left of the tracks. DANIEL E. FRIZANE COLLECTION.

Above: From 1939 on, the CA&E followed the east bank of the Fox River from the Aurora Avenue stop south to the new Aurora terminal on New York Avenue. Conditions permitting, this made for some scenic interurban viewing. On June 27, 1957, one of the steel cars is adjacent to the Fox River on its last lap into Aurora. GORDON E. LLOYD / RICHARD ALLERMANN COLLECTION.

Below: In 1940, Pullman car #411 is heading north, leaving Aurora and approaching Illinois Avenue. Prior to 1920, the track on the left took cars up to Broadway where they operated on street trackage. BARNEY NEUBURGER / RICHARD ALLERMANN COLLECTION.

Cincinnati car #430 has just pulled into the Aurora terminal and discharged its passengers. The wooden walkway to New York Street was built in later years when the CA&E gave up its storefront terminal on Broadway. To the rear you can see the short Aurora terminal siding where extra cars were stored. GREG HEIER COLLECTION.

The double track with trolley wire operation continued south along the east bank of the Fox River. Until the end of passenger operations, there were still a few passenger trains that utilized this double track section for meets. The next stop was at the crossing of Illinois Avenue, only one minute running time from Aurora Avenue.

Prior to 1920, the CA&E trains would turn east to Broadway (Hwy. 25) and operate on the street, sharing tracks with the local streetcars and other interurbans. In August of 1904, the AE&C leased a store at the corner of Fox Street and Broadway. The newspapers referred to this as a transfer station since it permitted AE&C passengers to transfer to city cars as well as interurban cars from other companies. As business increased, the AE&C decided that a more substantial facility was necessary. Hence, on September 14, 1915, the new terminal at Main and Broadway opened and became somewhat of a landmark for the company. Both the transfer station and the terminal were store front facilities that required passengers to board the interurban cars while they were operating down the center of Broadway. Two other interurban lines used the AE&C terminal in Aurora. The Joliet, Plainfield & Aurora operated southeast from Aurora while the Chicago, Aurora & DeKalb operated west from Aurora.

After 1920, the CA&E track continued south along the river and soon encountered another spring switch which returned the line to single track operation. A little bridge carried the line over Indian Creek, and some sidings to the east served the CA&E's Aurora freight house.

Between 1920 and 1939 the track headed to Broadway at this point to operate on the the tracks of the local street car line. This effectively reduced but did not eliminate street running during this period. A major improvement program in 1939 eliminated this last street operation of the CA&E, with the last car running on Aurora streets on December 31, 1939. After that date the single track continued south along the edge of the river and terminated at a modern, high level platform just north of New York Street. This was not exactly downtown Aurora, but the modern platform and the lack of street operation had its advantages. Just north of the platform was the short Aurora Terminal siding, where a few cars were stored overnight.

The total distance from Chicago's Wells Street Terminal to the Aurora Terminal was about 40 miles. Most CA&E trains required only 75 minutes for this trip. During the 1940's, when hourly headway was maintained, mid-day trains arrived in Aurora at 20 minutes past the hour. The crew had only ten minutes to change ends and head back to Chicago at 30 minutes after the hour. After the cutback in service to Forest Park in 1953, the headway was reduced to 90 minutes. Mid-day trains arrived in Aurora at 17 and 47 minutes past the hour, and then had a full 43 minutes to change ends before heading back to Chicago on the hour and half hour.

Above: **Pullman #401** heads a two-car fan trip which appears to include one of the ex-WB&A cars. The location is at the CB&Q overpass near Broadway and Benton, the southernmost point ever reached by CA&E trains. This street trackage on Broadway was removed shortly after the new terminal opened in late 1939. DANIEL E. FRIZANE COLLECTION.

Preceding Page: St. Louis car #452 is apparently transferring some packages to a waiting van. The new concrete and steel Aurora terminal with its high level platform could easily be mistaken for a modern rapid transit stop. LARRY PLACHNO COLLECTION.

Below: **July 3, 1949,** found St. Louis car #456 on the Aurora siding apparently ready to return to the main line. Abandonment of passenger service came exactly eight years later. MALCOLM MCCARTER / RICHARD ALLERMANN COLLECTION.

Sunset Lines • 107

10

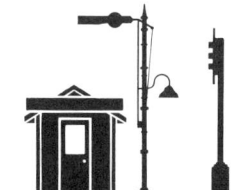

Batavia Branch

The Batavia branch was first placed in service in October of 1902 and hence was the first branch line built for the AE&C. After the demise of the Geneva branch in 1937, the Batavia branch was easily considered the least patronized and perhaps the least sophisticated of all CA&E passenger operations. In spite of this, the Batavia branch lasted until the end of passenger service.

The Batavia branch extended 5.9 miles from Batavia Junction on the Aurora branch to the community of Batavia on the Fox River. As originally constructed in 1902, the Batavia branch had ¾-mile of double track at the power house and 700 feet of double track at the Batavia terminal. In addition, there were substantial switching and storage tracks at the power house to accommodate the hopper cars of coal used to generate power. By 1930, the power house no longer generated its own power and this branch was essentially single track in later years as the only sidings were at the old Batavia Power House. Early records seem to indicate that the major reason for constructing the Batavia branch was to provide access to the power house since no appreciable passenger traffic was expected. Later, after the construction of Glenwood Park, the branch was able to generate some excursion business. Once the patronage to Glenwood Park was gone, the branch settled down to a mundane existence where it apparently was not operated at a profit, but was kept in operation as a shuttle to feed the Aurora line.

Connection was made with the Aurora branch at Batavia Junction, approximately 33 miles west of Wells Street Terminal in Chicago. Originally called Eola Junction by virtue of nearby Eola Road and the town of Eola located about 1½ miles south, the name was changed to the more appropriate Batavia Junction a few years after operations started.

PRECEDING PAGE

Pullman car #417 sits patiently under the trolley wire at the Batavia terminal on April 2, 1957. Abandonment of the passenger service was only months away. The presence of a small crowd on the platform leads one to speculate that #417 will soon be departing to run the short shuttle trip to Batavia Junction. STEVE MICHAEL.

The station itself was located on the "wye" between the Aurora track and the Batavia track. Eola Junction was initially constructed with a typical low level platform but this was replaced in later years with a more substantial high level platform to facilitate passenger transfers between Batavia and Aurora cars. The Batavia branch side of the platform had space for only one car door and required some care on the part of Batavia branch motormen when stopping.

Leaving Batavia Junction, the Batavia car would operate along the single track third rail line to the northwest. The first stop was located at Bilter Road, about one mile from the Junction. Most trains were scheduled to cover this distance in two minutes.

Continuing northwest, the track passed from Du Page to Kane County and the next stop was located adjacent to Butterfield Road, which was a state highway. Hence, the stop was known as State Road. Only one minute was allowed on the schedule from Bilter Road, a distance of somewhat less than one mile. State Road was unusual in that it had trolley wire strung over the road crossing. This road right-of-way was so wide that a train stopping for passengers could not build up enough speed to coast across the roadway to reach the third rail on the other side. Hence, the short stretch of overhead trolley wire prevented a potentially embarrassing situation for the train crew.

Northwest of here, the track passed the outskirts of what was later to become the Fermi National Accelerator Laboratory area and crossed Indian Creek on a bridge. Starting a gentle turn to the west, the track reached Wagner Road and the stop by the same name. Most trains were given two minutes to cover the approximately one mile distance from State Road.

From here the track went almost due west and crossed Radant Road, site of a stop which had been discontinued at a very early date. The distance from Wagner Road to Radant Road was only 1,306 feet and Fred Radant owned the farm running the entire distance between the two points. This close proximity is undoubtedly the major reason why the Radant Road stop was discontinued so early, only a few years after the branch opened. The next stop was located adjacent to Hart Road and normally required two minutes on the schedule from Wagner Road.

Above: Operations on the Batavia branch consisted almost exclusively of a single car which shuttled between Batavia and Batavia Junction, meeting Chicago trains on the Aurora branch. In a somewhat classic pose taken on July 14, 1954, Pullman car #411 from Forest Park to Aurora stopped at Batavia Junction and was transferring passengers to Jewett car #318 on the Batavia branch. Note that a portion of the high level platform had been flipped back to permit passage of a freight train. ROBERT SELLE / RICHARD ALLERMANN COLLECTION.

Below: This view looks west from Batavia Junction and shows the start of the Batavia branch. This photo was taken in 1962 during the scrapping operations, and the third rail had already been knocked over prior to removing the rail. It does show the rather short high level platform for Batavia branch trains and the edge that could be flipped up to allow passage of conventional freight cars. GREG HEIER.

Beyond Hart Road the track began turning northwest again, and passed beneath the CB&Q tracks. In earlier days, this line had actually been the main line of the CB&Q. Prior to building their own line between Chicago and Aurora, the CB&Q used this line north from Aurora to reach the C&NW tracks at West Chicago and then operated over the C&NW to reach Chicago.

Almost immediately the track passed under Illinois Highway 25 and began heading north along the Fox River. Going under the bridges, it was obvious that this remaining track was offset to one side. The bridge had originally been built to accommodate two tracks but the second track had been removed earlier. Most of the right-of-way west of Wheaton had been designed so that a second track could be added if traffic warranted. This was one of the few places where a second track had been installed and subsequently removed.

Just north of Highway 25, the Glenwood Park stop was located opposite the old Batavia Power House. In April of 1904, the interurban opened a company park at Glenwood which generated considerable business from Chicago. A high level platform was located at Glenwood in these earlier years so that Chicago "L" cars could be used to carry patrons to the park. During the early years there were substantial movements of special trains, many with Metropolitan "L" cars, taking Chicago residents out to enjoy Glenwood Park for the day. Most regular trains were given two minutes to reach Glenwood Park from Hart Road.

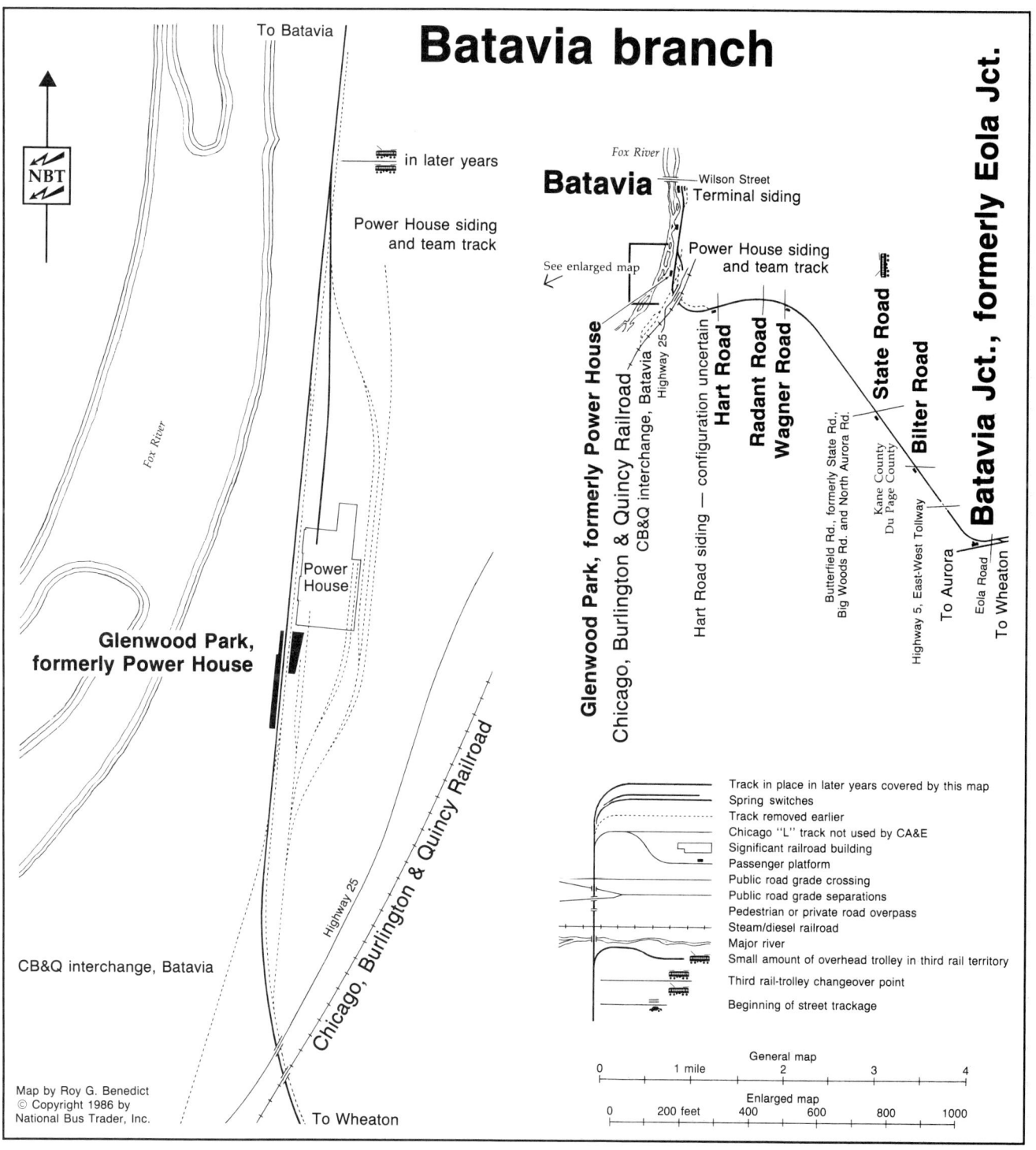

Sunset Lines • 111

Above: Were it not for the third rail, the Batavia branch could easily be mistaken for a less-sophisticated trolley line. The first stop on the branch beyond Batavia Junction was here at Bilter Road. Crossing protection consisted only of crossbucks and the stop was nothing more than a shanty, although the omnipresent CA&E passenger stop indicator is obvious. This photo was taken on March 28, 1957, during the final months of passenger operation. PAUL STRINGHAM / RICHARD ALLERMANN COLLECTION.

Below: A pair of former North Shore cars, headed by #137, pose at the State Road crossing while apparently on an excursion trip. State Road was so wide, and the corresponding gap in the third rail so long, that this short section of trolley wire had been installed to prevent a car from being stranded powerless over the roadway. The overhead wire was normally used only by cars which made a passenger stop westbound at State Road. DANIEL E. FRIZANE COLLECTION.

Most passengers on the Batavia branch rode from Batavia to Batavia Junction while patronage at the intermediate stops was minimal. The passenger facilities provided at these intermediate stops reflected this lack of patronage. *Above:* The Wagner Road stop was the next stop beyond State Road. *Below:* In later years, Hart Road was the next stop beyond Wagner Road. Both stops rated nothing more than a cozy shelter, a short passenger platform and the traditional passenger signal.
BOTH PHOTOS BY GREG HEIER

Sunset Lines • 113

Above: **Just before reaching the Fox River on the south side of Batavia, the track passed under the dual bridges of Highway 25 and the Chicago Burlington & Quincy Railroad. On July 3, 1948, St. Louis car #457 posed at this location while on a railfan excursion.** MALCOLM MCCARTER / RICHARD ALLERMANN COLLECTION.

Below: **CA&E cars #10 and #319 were used on a fan trip in 1939. This location was immediately south of the Batavia Power House and the Glenwood Park stop. The dual smokestacks appear above the power house while the Glenwood Park stop is on the far left.** RICHARD ALLERMANN COLLECTION.

This photo shows a closer view of the Glenwood Park stop and its passenger signal. On the opposite side of the tracks is the Batavia Power House. Car #20 was apparently running as an extra and may have been used on an early fan trip.
DANIEL E. FRIZANE COLLECTION.

Sidings were located at the power house and apparently were used as late as the 1940's for an infrequent meet on the branch. In earlier years, an interchange with the CB&Q was located immediately to the south to provide coal for the power house. During the 1920's, conventional railroad cars were received at this interchange and delivered to other points on the interurban. However, use of the power house diminished during the 1920's and the interchange was eventually taken out when the CA&E no longer needed coal for the power house, probably during the 1930's. After this interchange was removed, there was little movement of conventional railroad freight cars over the Batavia branch.

Trains continued almost directly north from Glenwood Park, and in later years, switched from third rail to trolley just north of the power house. As originally constructed, the Batavia branch had third rail power all the way into the Batavia station platform. The single track continued along the east bank of the Fox River and terminated at the high level platform at Wilson Street in Batavia. In earlier years, a second track was provided at the Batavia terminal for those rare occasions when more than one train would be in Batavia. Initially, a barn-like open-ended structure provided shelter over the platforms, but this was torn down in later years. Most trains were scheduled for 9 or 10 minutes for the 5.9 miles from Batavia Junction to Batavia.

Of all the CA&E operations, the Batavia branch was one of the least changed over the years. With the exception of the stop at Radant Road, it appears that all stops instituted in 1902 when the branch opened remained in service until the end. Trolley wire was put up from the power house to the end of the line in about 1930 as a safety measure, and the power house as well as the CB&Q interchange diminished in importance after the 1920's. Other than this, operations on the branch remained virtually unchanged for 55 years.

Records seem to indicate that carload freight service was provided over the Batavia branch in the 1920's. However, the branch had no sidings other than the power house and it appears that CA&E freight trains had no need to serve the branch after the CB&Q interchange was removed.

It is interesting to note that Batavia was the only Fox River community served by the CA&E where no connection was made with the trolley lines of the Fox River Division. At Batavia, the CA&E track was located on the east bank of the river while the Fox River interurban line (and most of the community) was located on the west side.

Unlike the other CA&E Fox River branches, most service on the Batavia branch was provided by a shuttle car which met Aurora trains at Batavia Junction and did not operate as a through car into Chicago. There are indications that lightweight car #500 was originally purchased for service on the Batavia branch in an early effort to reduce operating costs, but the car burned out its motors and in general did not work out. Later years usually saw one of the older wooden cars on the Batavia shuttle, perhaps the only regular assignment of wood equipment west of Wheaton in the railroad's last years.

Above: Between the power house siding and the Batavia station, CA&E trains used overhead trolley wire instead of third rail. The trolley wire and unimpressive right-of-way at this location yields a view somewhat more in keeping with a typical Midwestern interurban rather than the CA&E's traditional high-speed operations. From the age of the autos, one might surmise that car #20 was running an earlier single-car fantrip. DANIEL E. FRIZANE COLLECTION.

Below: Car #16 strikes a somewhat typical interurban pose at the high level Batavia station platform while awaiting departure time. The station itself was located on Wilson Street, to the rear of the train. Car #16 was frequently assigned to the Batavia shuttle runs during the 1940's. DANIEL E. FRIZANE COLLECTION.

On August 31, 1942, this two-car fantrip was parked in the old Batavia terminal siding, immediately south of the Batavia station. Car #137 had been acquired from the North Shore Line. DANIEL E. FRIZANE COLLECTION.

Through the 1940's there was one through car from Batavia to Chicago which was connected to the morning Cannonball at Wheaton. All other Batavia trips of this period were run by a shuttle car which came from Wheaton at the start of the day and returned to Wheaton at the end of the day.

Operations on the Batavia branch were very interesting throughout the 1940's. The morning car left Wheaton at 5:00 a.m. and operated a scheduled deadhead trip to Batavia in 30 minutes. One might assume that passengers on this trip were minimal. At 5:50 the car left Batavia for a shuttle run to Batavia Junction to meet an Aurora train bound for Chicago. Shuttle trips ran every 25-30 minutes in the rush hour, giving the crew only a few minutes at each end to turn around. However, turning the shuttle car at each end of the line was not a major task in earlier years since the crew had only one car length to walk and no trolley poles to pull as both ends of the Batavia branch were equipped with third rail.

The trip leaving Batavia at 7:16 a.m. did operate through to Wheaton and connected with the morning Cannonball. After the morning rush hour, operations on the branch were one step above boredom. With hourly service on the Aurora branch, mid-day Batavia cars left Batavia at 26 or 28 minutes after the hour and took 11 to 13 minutes to reach Batavia Junction. Here, the shuttle car transferred passengers to a Chicago-bound train from Aurora which left Batavia Junction at 39 minutes past the hour. The crew would sit at the Junction for 30 minutes, waiting for the arrival of the train from Chicago to Aurora at 9 minutes past the hour. Since Batavia Junction was rather isolated, one might surmise that the regular crew caught up on their reading or found some other means to pass the time while sitting out in the middle of nowhere. One report indicates that the regular Batavia shuttle car crew took to cultivating a vegetable garden in the summer months. This was located just west of the station in the "wye" between the tracks. After receiving connecting passengers, the car would leave for Batavia and arrive there at 20 minutes after the hour. The crew now had 6 or 8 minutes to change ends and head back to Batavia Junction to meet the next Chicago train.

If this schedule seems a little tight on the Batavia end, it can be easily explained by looking at the distance from Batavia Junction to both Batavia and Aurora. The distance from Batavia Junction to Aurora was 5.0 miles and trains were normally scheduled for 9 minutes. By comparison, the distance from Batavia Junction to Batavia was 5.9 miles, which was scheduled for 11 to 13 minutes. Many people were not aware that the Batavia branch was actually longer than the distance from Batavia Junction to Aurora. It might also be noted that the tracks on the Batavia branch were not as well maintained and did not permit the speeds that the main line to Aurora permitted.

The evening schedule during the 1940's kept the shuttle car busy meeting Chicago trains. The last train from Chicago left Wells Street at 12:30 a.m. and made a connection with the Batavia car at Batavia Junction at 1:27 a.m. This car reached Batavia at 1:38. At 1:40 a.m. it left Batavia and made a scheduled deadhead run back to Wheaton, closing out Batavia branch service until the morning car arrived after 5:00 a.m.

After 1953, when service was cut back to Forest Park, rail service on the Batavia branch was reduced to weekday rush hours only with all trips (except for pull-outs and pull-ins to Wheaton) being shuttles to Batavia Junction. Mid-day and weekend service to Batavia was provided by extending the CA&E motor coach service from St. Charles and Geneva to Batavia.

When passenger service ended in 1957, the CA&E was still providing 7 weekday round trips in the morning on the Batavia branch and 7 in the evening.

After the end of passenger service, the new East-West Illinois Tollway cut the Batavia branch at grade between Batavia Junction and Bilter Road in 1958. The Illinois Tollway Authority had officially purchased 200 feet of the Batavia branch right-of-way for this purpose under an arrangement that perpetuated CA&E passenger service for a brief period. Although a bridge had been hinted at, this bisection of the line most likely would have created difficulties to any resumption of operations on the branch if indeed the CA&E had found a way to resurrect its passenger service.

11

Elgin Branch

The Elgin branch consisted of a single track line and occasional short passing sidings between Wheaton and Elgin. This branch was placed in service on Tuesday, May 29, 1903, approximately 9 months after service on the branch to Aurora the and main line to Laramie had opened. Original plans had been to open the branch at an earlier date but a lack of materials had delayed construction of the line.

It is well to remember that both the Elgin and Aurora branches did not provide a direct route to Chicago but rather a substantial "dog leg" via Wheaton. Direct service between Elgin and Chicago by the Milwaukee Road operated substantially north of the CA&E line. In similar fashion, direct service by the CB&Q between Aurora and Chicago operated considerably south of the CA&E's line. One might assume that the AE&C management felt this disadvantage would be overcome by more frequent and cleaner service.

The single track Elgin branch diverged on the north side of the Wheaton yards and made a sweeping turn to the north while climbing a fill to rise over Liberty Drive on a small through girder bridge and upward to reach a substantial bridge over the Chicago & North Western's Galena Division tracks. This bridge involved three through girder spans and a thru truss span, and was the longest bridge on the Chicago Aurora & Elgin. In order to open the Elgin branch in 1903, a wooden trestle was constructed over the C&NW tracks. The steel sections were added several years later, probably in 1909 when the massive bridge over the EJ&E in West Chicago was constructed.

Immediately north of the bridge was the Wesley Street stop. The tracks then began turning northwest past the Lincoln Avenue stop and across Winfield Creek. The track then continued straight past the Jewel Road stop to Geneva Junction. This was the junction with the Geneva branch and warranted both a siding and a station while the branch was operational. Some of the Geneva cars were attached and detached from Elgin cars at this point. Other Geneva cars operated on their own to Wheaton where they were connected to Aurora or Wheaton trains.

Only a short distance away was the stop known as Pleasant Hill, located 2.4 miles from Wheaton. After the abandonment of the Geneva branch, the Geneva Junction stop was eliminated while the nearby Pleasant Hill stop retained a siding and was the end of the first signal block beyond Wheaton. During the early 1940's, Pleasant Hill was dropped from public schedule folders but was retained in the employees' timetable until the end.

Continuing northwest from Pleasant Hill siding, the track soon crossed the intersection of Geneva Road and County Farm Road. The Geneva Road station was located just beyond the intersection. After the CA&E was abandoned, County Farm Road was re-aligned at this point to eliminate a slight "dog leg" at the intersection caused by avoiding the CA&E tracks.

Beyond Geneva Road it seemed as though civilization was left behind as the track headed through a forest preserve and was soon passing along and then crossing the West Branch of the Du Page River. Emerging from the forest preserve, the track soon reached Prince Crossing Road. This stop was located 5.1 miles from Wheaton and required 6 to 8 minutes running time. Prince Crossing was a relatively important location although it normally did not generate a great deal of passenger traffic. In addition to the station, the operator ran the Ingalton substation and also was responsible for setting the train order signal and passing train orders to the crew. A small siding was located here for the substation. At one point in the early years of the AE&C, twenty acres of land was acquired west of Prince Crossing as a possible site for a shops complex. The land remained unused and unsold at least until the 1950's.

Still headed northwest, the CA&E track left the Prince Crossing stop and soon passed beneath the Chicago Great Western. Interestingly, this was the same railroad track which paralleled the CA&E between Maywood and Elmhurst. However, while the CGW ran virtually arrow-straight, the CA&E took a large "detour" via Wheaton.

PRECEDING PAGE

Car #425, inbound from Elgin, emerges from the C&NW bridge and begins the long, sweeping curve down to the main line. The date was May 23, 1948. GORDON E. LLOYD / LARRY PLACHNO COLLECTION.

Sunset Lines • 119

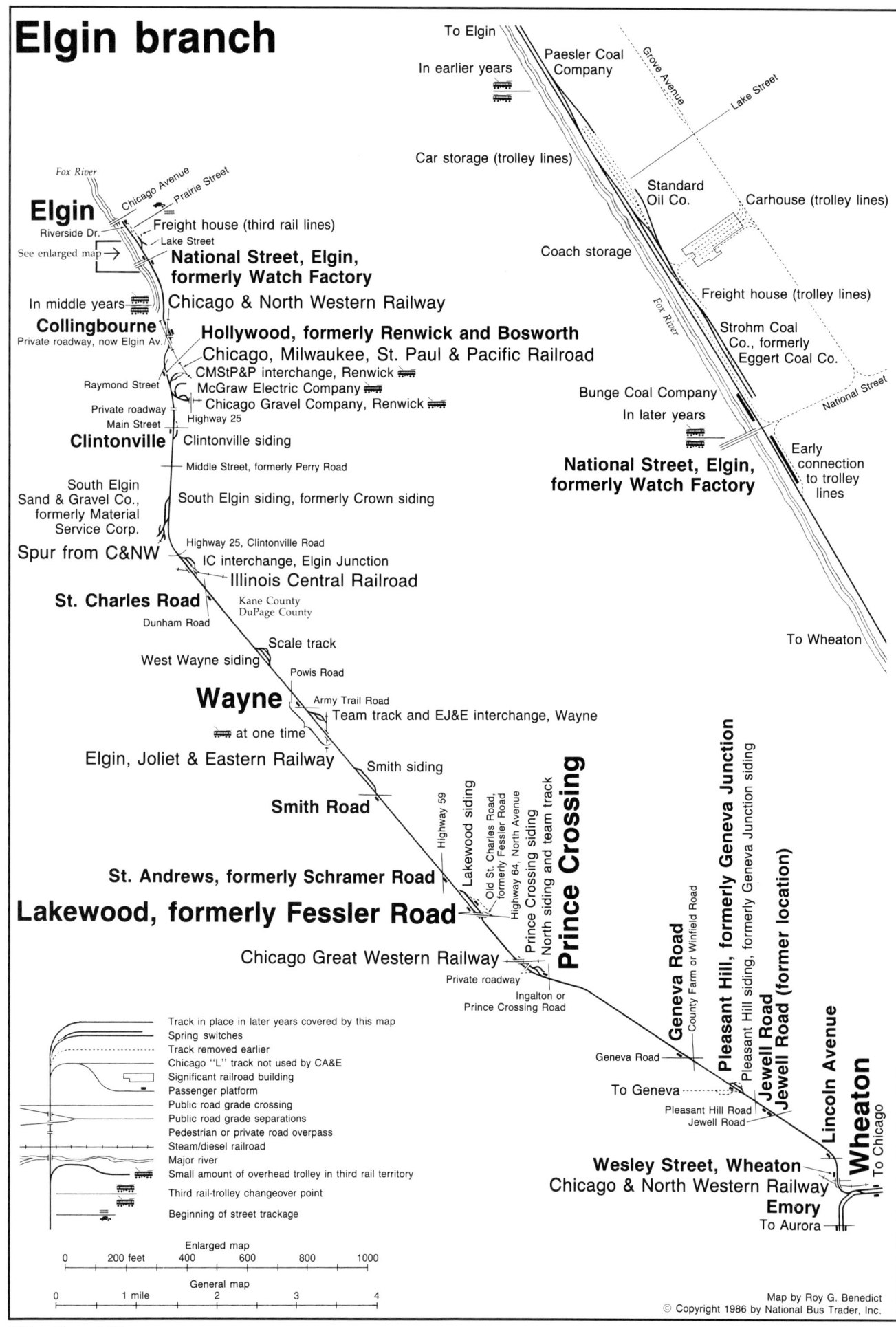

Above: **This is where the Elgin branch started. Cincinnati car #429 has just taken the switch from the main line at the entrance to the Wheaton yard, passed the interlocking tower, and started up the grade toward the Liberty Drive and C&NW bridges. The tracks in the foreground are storage tracks at the north end of CA&E's Wheaton yard.** GREG HEIER / DANIEL E. FRIZANE COLLECTION.

Below: **In November of 1955, CA&E Pullman car #410 is inbound from Elgin as it crosses the "High Bridge" over the Chicago & North Western. The photographer is looking north and the car is heading towards the camera. The Chicago & North Western tracks are visible below the bridge.** DONALD R. KAPLAN / SHORE LINE INTERURBAN HISTORICAL SOCIETY.

Above: The Price Crossing station was located adjacent to the crossing of Ingalton Road. The rather elaborate building was necessary because train orders were issued at this location and the Ingalton substation was located here. St. Louis car #452 is heading toward Wheaton and Chicago. DANIEL E. FRIZANE COLLECTION.

Preceding Page: The little Lincoln Avenue stop was located on the north side of Wheaton. Behind the car, the tracks turned heading northwest toward Elgin. CA&E Pullman car #406 was inbound from Elgin on July 16, 1956. JAMES BARRICK / RICHARD ALLERMANN COLLECTION.

Below: The Lakewood Station was one of the more important stops on the Elgin branch. Passengers transferred here to CA&E buses for St. Charles and Geneva while passenger trains could meet on the passing siding. On February 4, 1956, car #415 was heading to Chicago and was accepting passengers from the connecting CA&E bus. GORDON E. LLOYD / LARRY PLACHNO COLLECTION.

Above: On Sunday December 16, 1945, two of the new St. Louis cars (#451 and #453) were on Smith Road siding, possibly to meet a regular car from Elgin to Chicago. As the photo shows, there was no residential development in the immediate area. Consequently, Smith Road was more important for its passing siding than for its passenger count. EDWARD FRANK / RICHARD ALLERMANN COLLECTION.

Shortly, the track went through an underpass under North Avenue (Illinois Highway 64) and into the Lakewood Station. This is one stop which substantially increased in importance over the years. Located approximately 6.1 miles from Wheaton, it took most CA&E trains 7 to 10 minutes to reach this point.

Lakewood did not become important until 1937, when it was designated as the rail-to-motor coach transfer point for the CA&E buses which replaced the Geneva branch by providing service to St. Charles and Geneva. The CA&E buses turned, received and discharged passengers in a parking lot on the west side of the tracks adjacent to the station.

In the late 1920's, this stop was initially established at the grade crossing with Fessler Road. The road became more important in later years as an extension of Chicago's North Avenue. It was later put on an overpass over the CA&E tracks when it became designated as Illinois Highway 64. In the late 1930's this stop was known as "St. Charles-Geneva Transfer" and it was not until the 1940's that the "Lakewood" name appeared in CA&E timetables. Lakewood was named after a nearby subdivision. A long double-ended passing siding with spring switches was built at this location and soon became the preferred point for meets on the Elgin branch. By the time the last CA&E timetable went into effect in 1953, passenger train meets on the Elgin branch were scheduled only during rush hours, and all were scheduled to take place at this point. Lakewood, expectedly, was the end of the second block signal section beyond Wheaton.

Going beyond the end of the Lakewood passing siding, trains returned to single track heading northwest. Only one minute of running time was permitted from Lakewood to the St. Andrews stop. Located just prior to the crossing of Illinois Highway 59, the St. Andrews stop was named for the St. Andrews Golf Course, located just north of the tracks.

After leaving St. Andrews, trains crossed the highway and had one minute to reach the Smith Road stop, located near the intersection of Smith and Munger Roads. Smith siding, double ended but not equipped with spring switches, was located just north of this stop. This stop and siding went through just the opposite situation as Lakewood; it started out as an important location on the AE&C but declined through the years.

The Smith Road stop was put in place when service started on the Elgin branch in 1903. Early records indicate that the Smith Road stop was used by many trains, if only because several trains used the siding for meets. About 1945, after the Lakewood stop became more important, the number of trains stopping at Smith Road was drastically reduced to only two or three trains in each direction, although the siding was still in use for meets.

PRECEDING PAGE

One day in April, 1956, a photographer standing on the Highway 64 overpass was able to record this scene of congestion at Lakewood. No less than four CA&E movements were at Lakewood at the same time. From left to right we see: the regular CA&E bus; freight locomotives #4006-4005 pulling a short freight towards Wheaton; following it is a wooden passenger car on a fan trip; car #419 heads toward Elgin on a regular run.
DOUG CHRISTIANSEN / RICHARD ALLERMANN COLLECTION.

Above: Wayne was the only community with any significant population on the Elgin branch between Wheaton and Elgin. The little station was located just north of the EJ&E interchange and adjacent to Army Trail Road. Here, locomotives #4006-4005 with a freight train pass the station heading northwest to Elgin. GREG HEIER.

Below: Jewett Car #318 poses on the Wayne scale track siding while a westbound four-car scheduled train highballs past on the main line. The date was July, 1949, and the occasion was a railfan excursion. VICTOR G. WAGNER.

A CA&E steel car rolls across Dunham Road, just west of the Du Page-Kane County line. The St. Charles Road stop was located to the right of the photographer. The stop got its name because Dunham Road did head in the direction of St. Charles.
T. HEFNER / LARRY KOSTKA COLLECTION.

At least one source indicates that Smith siding was equipped with spring switches through World War II to facilitate meets, but that they were removed when the Lakewood siding assumed greater importance. With the new 1953 schedule, all passenger train meets were moved to the Lakewood siding, possibly because of the spring switches and motor coach connection at that point.

Continuing northwest from Smith siding, the CA&E track soon crossed over the EJ&E track on an overpass, and just beyond was a lead to the EJ&E interchange. After passing Army Trail Road, trains would stop at Wayne. Located 9.5 miles and about 14 minutes out of Wheaton, Wayne was the only community of measurable size between Wheaton and Elgin. In this respect, it was somewhat comparable to Warrenville on the Aurora branch. The 1930 census placed Wayne's population at only 225.

Northwest of Wayne, the CA&E track entered the Pratts-Wayne Woods, which was the location of the West Wayne siding and scale track. The siding was $^9/_{10}$ of a mile beyond Wayne and 10.4 miles beyond Wheaton. No stop was located here, as the scale track was used by the freight trains which frequently operated on this part of the line. The West Wayne siding contained room for 24 cars and was a favorite spot for freight trains to "take siding" when passenger trains were due. At this point the C&NW's West Chicago-Elgin line approached very close to the west.

West Wayne was also the end of the third signal block section beyond Wheaton.

After the West Wayne siding and scale track, the CA&E line emerged from the woods, crossed a small creek, and then crossed the county line from Du Page to Kane County. The St. Charles Road stop was located just beyond at Dunham Road. For the sake of clarity, it might be mentioned that Dunham Road was originally called St. Charles road and did in fact go southwest to St. Charles. The name of the road was later changed but the CA&E retained the earlier name for its stop at this location. This stop was about 15 minutes from Wheaton and had a history very much like the Smith Road stop. The St. Charles Road stop was established when the Elgin branch was put in service in 1903. It remained a regular stop on all but the most important trains until the mid-1940's, when only one train in each direction continued to stop here. The last schedule, in 1953, added two more westbound trains.

Leaving St. Charles Road, the CA&E track continued northwest and climbed to an overpass over the Illinois Central tracks. Immediately beyond this was the CA&E-IC interchange, which was known as Elgin Junction. At this point, the CA&E track was opposite Coleman but on the east side of the Fox River. About 1½ miles west (and across the river) was the famous Coleman interchange between the IC and Fox River lines, which kept a small segment of the Fox River trolley trackage in operation as a freight carrier.

Above: **A CA&E steel car on the Elgin branch just north of the Illinois Central overpass. The bridge over the IC tracks can be seen in the distance and the IC interchange is on the left. The third rail is on the left side of the track but is difficult to see because it blends in with the nearest running rail.** DANIEL E. FRIZANE COLLECTION.

Below: **Locomotives #4005-4006 are pointing north at the bridge crossing over Highway 25. The train is obviously switching cars at the Illinois Central interchange which is just on the other side of the tracks at this point. A small creek also crossed under the CA&E next to Highway 25.** GREG HEIER.

Above: CA&E locomotives #3003-3004 are switching at the South Elgin Sand and Gravel Co. between the IC interchange and Clintonville. The CA&E Elgin branch main line is on the left and the two locomotives are pointing north. This early photo shows both locomotives in their original black paint scheme. Beyond the tipple, to the right, non-electrified tracks continued to a C&NW branch line. GREG HEIER COLLECTION.

Below: Clintonville was another of those station buildings built to greater proportions that its patronage would normally dictate. The reason for the larger station was a substation at this point and the fact that the Clintonville operator also issued train orders. Car #415, the regular Elgin schedule, meets wooden car #318 on the short Clintonville siding. #318 was obviously being used on a fan excursion. LARRY PLACHNO COLLECTION.

Above: **Just north of Clintonville, a southbound two-car train from Elgin (headed by Cincinnati car #423) passes a group of sidings commonly known as Renwick. Locomotives #3002-3003 are busy switching the Milwaukee Road interchange. Other sidings in the area served the Toastmaster Plant and the gravel pit.** TRUMAN HEFNER / LARRY KOSTKA COLLECTION.

Below: **This unusual photo shows a CA&E car approaching Elgin from the south. In the immediate foreground is the Milwaukee Road crossing while you can see the Raymond St. crossing and the Hollywood stop in the background. The Collingbourne stop is only a few feet behind the photographer. The photo was taken from a private road overpass immediately south of the Collingbourne stop.** GREG HEIER COLLECTION.

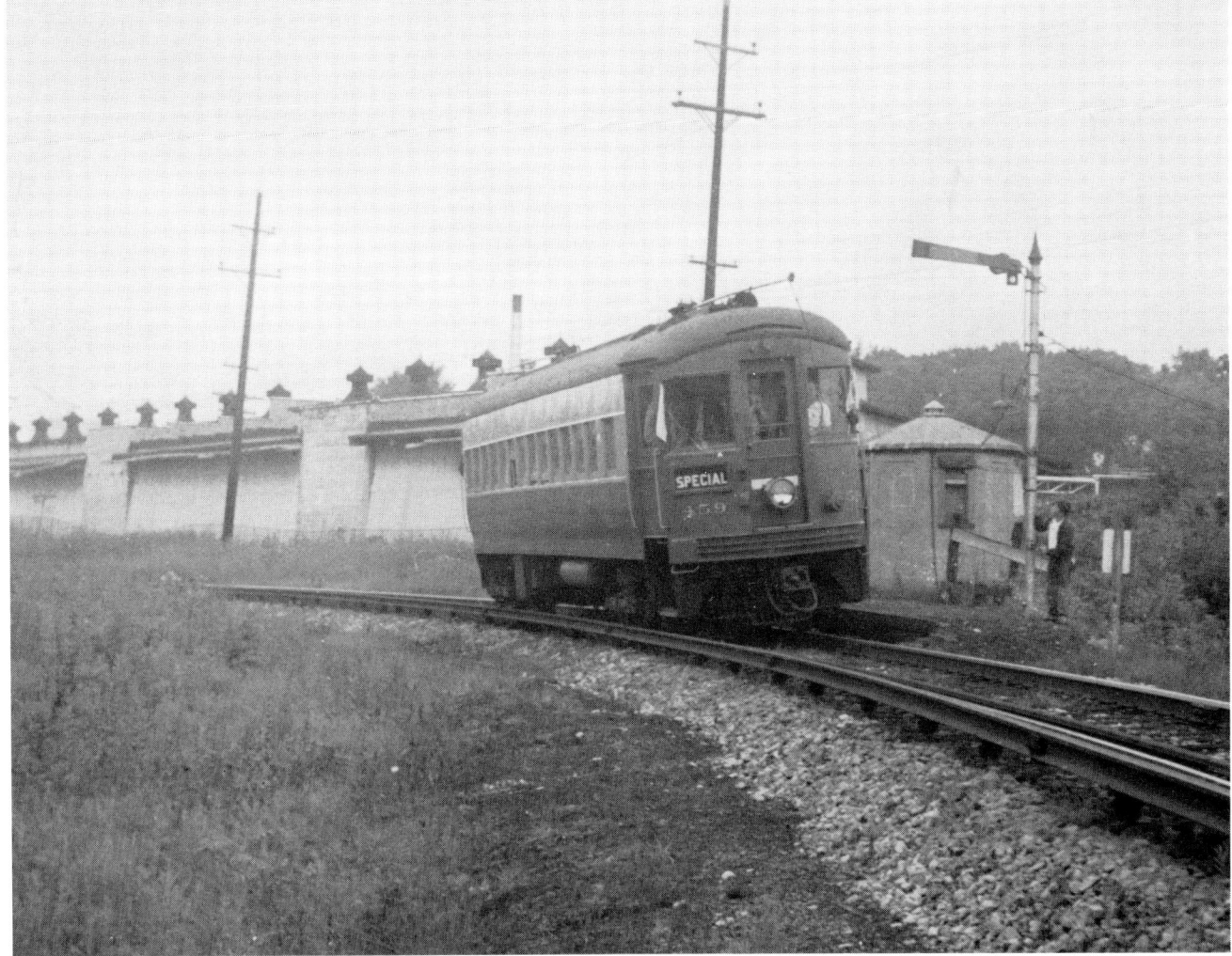

The stop at Collingbourne was little more than a wide spot in the right-of-way on a sweeping curve between the Milwaukee Road underpass and the C&NW underpass. St. Louis car #459 pauses at Collingbourne on a fan trip in 1954. One member of the group is apparently setting the passenger stop signal for the photographers. RICHARD ALLERMANN COLLECTION.

Continuing past the IC interchange, the track crossed Illinois Highway 25 on an overpass and then made a long turn to head almost directly north while returning to street level. To the west was the South Elgin siding, which also served the local gravel pit and provided an unofficial and somewhat impractical connection with a Chicago & North Western branch. Slightly further north was the Clintonville stop and a single-ended siding.

Clintonville was located 13.2 miles and about 18-19 minutes from Wheaton. It was also 4 miles and 5 minutes beyond Wayne. Clintonville was another of those stops with a station size all out of proportion to its patronage. However, the building also served to house a substation and the operator was responsible for setting the train order signal and making out train orders for the crews. In later years, with the virtual elimination of the St. Charles Road stop, the Wayne-Clintonville segment became the longest run for CA&E trains west of Wheaton without a stop. Clintonville was also the end of the fourth signal block from Wheaton.

North of Clintonville, the CA&E began dropping into the Fox River Valley. You could see some freight sidings on the east side of the track which served a gravel pit, the Toastmaster plant of McGraw Edison, and also provided a connection with the Milwaukee Road at this point. These sidings were unusual in that some portions were powered by trolley wire instead of third rail.

Immediately beyond the sidings was the Hollywood stop, which was known as Renwick in the earlier days. The CA&E track then crossed Raymond Steeet and Poplar Creek, followed by a long "S" curve to the right crossing under the Milwaukee Road tracks. The Collingbourne stop was located where the "S" curve reversed itself.

Leaving Collingbourne, the CA&E track crossed under the C&NW line to emerge on the east bank of the Fox River. This area is directly across the river from the State Mental Hospital, and in later years the new Highway 20 bypass would be built overhead.

Continuing north along the Fox River, the CA&E had an important stop at National Street near the famous Elgin Watch Factory. Records indicate that there was a connection between the AE&C and the streetcar lines at National Street in earlier years. Through cars, such as the North Shore charter to Rockford and through operation of the "Carolyn," probably used this connection. At National Street, the conductor would put up the trolley pole since Elgin branch trackage north of here was powered by trolley wire and not third rail.

Sunset Lines • 131

Above: **North of National Street, cars switched from third rail power to trolley poles. Here, locomotives #4005-4006 are busy hauling a freight train south along the river. In the distance is the famous Elgin Watch factory and National Street.** GREG HEIER.

Below: **In earlier days, the third rail extended north of National Street and a connection was made with the Fox River Trolley Division at this point. In 1934, Aurora Elgin & Fox River car #303 and locomotive #49 were "parked" alongside the CA&E main line, as were a few of the CA&E's own passenger cars. The Fox River is to the left in this photo looking north.** RICHARD ALLERMANN COLLECTION.

132 • *Sunset Lines*

Above: CA&E car #401 heads south from the Elgin terminal along the Fox River. The car is north of National Street and approximately adjacent to the old car house connection with the Fox River lines. A Milwaukee Road train can be seen across the Fox River on the west side. DANIEL E. FRIZANE COLLECTION.

Below: A two-car train headed by Cincinnati Car #420 awaits its departure time at the Elgin terminal. In the background the Chicago Street bridge over the Fox River can be seen. In earlier days the terminal on Chicago Street was also used by the Elgin & Belvidere and the Fox River interurbans. GREG HEIER COLLECTION.

It's train time in Elgin as passengers board St. Louis car #456. This photo was probably taken soon after the St. Louis cars went into service as the car appears to have the initial paint scheme applied to these cars in 1945. After 1939, Elgin was the CA&E's only Fox River terminal without a high level platform. GREG HEIER COLLECTION.

Beyond National Street was the later connection to the Fox River Division trolley lines and several freight sidings. Eggert siding, with a capacity of 18 cars, was used to store some passenger cars overnight. Starting with the 1953 schedule, two evening (and one Saturday) train crews would leave their cars here after their runs for use by two commuter crews the next morning. All other crews and equipment ran back to Wheaton for overnight storage.

The single track continued north to a stub at the main Elgin Station just south of Chicago Street. In earlier years there were two stub end tracks, one on either side of the low-level platform. After 1939, Elgin was the only CA&E Fox River terminal with a low level platform. The last 1,000 feet of CA&E trackage into Elgin was laid on the right-of-way for a road in which the AE&C had obtained a franchise from the City of Elgin to operate. In later years this was not used as a street and the CA&E was able to use it as private right-of-way. Consequently, the CA&E was prohibited from constructing anything as substantial as a passenger platform on what was technically a street. The Elgin Station was actually a store front on Chicago Street and passengers left through the rear to board the trains.

PRECEDING PAGE

November of 1955 found car #404 at the end of the line in the Elgin terminal awaiting its departure time. The Fox River partially reflects the Pullman car along the shore. The staircase at the far left led up to the station on Chicago Street. DONALD R. KAPLAN / SHORE LINE INTERURBAN HISTORICAL SOCIETY.

For many years, the Elgin & Belvidere Electric shared this station with the CA&E. Passengers transferring from the CA&E to the E&B walked through the station and then boarded the waiting E&B connecting car in the middle of Chicago Street.

Elgin was located 16.2 miles from Wheaton, making it 2.3 miles longer than the Aurora branch at the end of service. Wheaton-to-Elgin required a running time of 22-24 minutes. Total running time from Wells Street Terminal in Chicago was 67 to 80 minutes for about 40 miles of track.

During the 1940's, the normal mid-day service to Elgin was hourly with trains arriving at 20 minutes past the hour. Crews had ten minutes to reverse seats and change ends before heading back to Chicago at 30 minutes past the hour. After service was cut back to Forest Park in 1953, the headway to Elgin was reduced to 90 minutes, with mid-day trains arriving alternately at 17 and 47 minutes after the hour. Because of the relaxed headway, crews now had about 40 minutes before returning east.

12

Geneva Branch

The Geneva branch was placed in service in 1909 and was abandoned in 1937. Hence, it held the somewhat dubious distinction of being the last line built to the Fox River and the first of them to be abandoned. The Geneva branch could also be considered CA&E's only significant abandonment prior to 1951 (the Westchester branch was abandoned in 1951 and was never operated by the CA&E, while the Cook County / Mt. Carmel branch remained in part for freight service).

Technically, the Geneva branch was built by the Chicago Wheaton & Western, another interurban line, which was later leased and eventually merged into the AE&C. In spite of the name, CW&W trackage never was built in either Chicago or Wheaton, although the trains on this line did reach both points.

The Geneva branch consisted of a single track line from Geneva Junction on the Elgin branch through West Chicago to Geneva on the Fox River, a distance of approximately 9.4 miles. Within a year after service started on the branch, AE&C trains were extended over 2 miles of Fox River trolley tracks to St. Charles, an arrangement which continued until the branch was abandoned. Normal service on the branch was usually provided with a single car.

Company records indicate that upon completion, the Geneva branch consisted of 9.35 main line miles, 0.40 miles of sidings, and 0.07 miles of industrial spurs. Research has failed to uncover any carload freight on the branch and it is assumed that the .07 miles of "industrial spurs" was probably either the Geneva Jct. or High Lake siding when considered as a team track.

In comparison with the other CA&E branches, the Geneva branch was always somewhat less important and had poorer construction. In addition, the Geneva branch had much more street and trolley wire operation than any other segment of the railroad. When hourly service was provided on the Elgin and Aurora branches, the Geneva branch had 90-minute headways. The Geneva branch was the segment of the railroad most like the traditional Midwestern interurban.

There were no substations located at any point between Geneva Junction and Geneva. As a consequence, the branch frequently suffered from a lack of power, and was considered one of the worst segments of the CA&E from this standpoint. It is known that a power line was constructed from the Ingalton substation to West Chicago, but this was primarily to supply commercial power for lighting to West Chicago.

The branch started at Geneva Junction, located 27.7 miles from Wells Street Terminal and 2.4 miles northwest of Wheaton. When timetables coincided with Elgin trains, the Geneva cars were connected or disconnected at Geneva Junction. At other times the Geneva cars would operate to and from Wheaton, where they were connected to or disconnected from Chicago trains. The frequency of service dictated that some Geneva trains would be attached to local trains between Wheaton and Chicago. After abandonment of the Geneva branch, Geneva Junction was removed and a new stop named Pleasant Hill was instituted in the same area.

Powered by third rail, the branch went west from Geneva Junction to the first stop at County Farm Road. The stop itself was called the Winfield Road stop.

Continuing west, the track crossed the West Branch of the Du Page River and entered a heavily wooded area which was later designated as a forest preserve. There was a small stop at Fanette which apparently was insignificant since it was not located near any major population center or road crossing. The first significant stop was at High Lake, serving the High Lake residential section. This is an area on the east side of West Chicago which was laid out in the 1920's. A dance hall and pavilion was also located near the station, but burned in the mid-1930's. A small but impressive passenger waiting shelter was located on a small hill to the north of the tracks.

PRECEDING PAGE

Between West Chicago and the Fox River, the Geneva branch had a rather open right-of-way and no substantial stops. This was probably the one section of the branch where the motorman could get his car up to the "company notch." CA&E Pullman car #412 heads away from the camera as it approaches Kress Road on a run to St. Charles. A. W. JOHNSON / RICHARD ALLERMANN COLLECTION.

Geneva branch

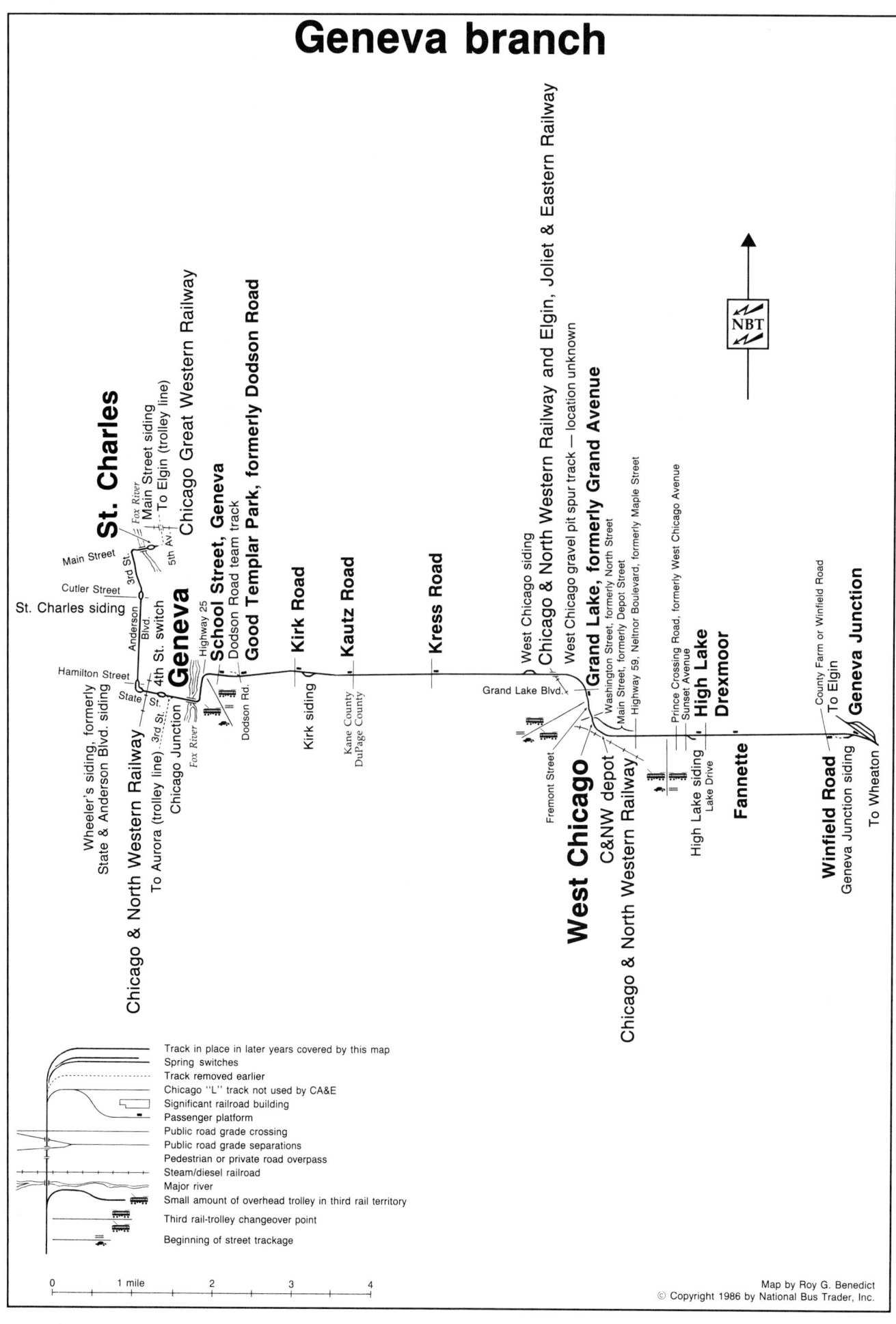

138 • Sunset Lines

Left: This view of Geneva Junction was taken in about 1936 and looks northwest. The photographer is standing on the Elgin branch main line while the switch to the right is for a siding. The Geneva branch cuts off to the left. Geneva Junction marked the end of the first signal block beyond Wheaton.

Above: The High Lake Station served a residential area on the east side of West Chicago. At this point the track was in a shallow cut and the station was located on the north side of the track with a very wide stairway leading down to track level. Although a small building, the station had high quality brick construction. GREG HEIER COLLECTION.

West Chicago was the only major community between Wheaton and the Fox River served by the CA&E. This was somewhat of a mixed blessing since the Chicago & North Western provided fast and frequent commuter service from West Chicago to Chicago. Abandonment of the Geneva branch was only hours away when CA&E Pullman car #403 passed the C&NW station on Main Street on October 30, 1937. The track and street curved to the north immediately behind the car. A. W. JOHNSON / RICHARD ALLERMAN COLLECTION.

Above: This view was photographed from the corner of Washington and Main, looking south on Main St. in West Chicago. The Chicago & North Western depot is obvious if you look down Main Street about two blocks. Pullman car #412 is making a stop at the CA&E station in West Chicago, which is to the extreme right of the photo. GEORGE KRAMBLES / GREG HEIER COLLECTION.

Below: On the northwest side of West Chicago, the CA&E tracks left city streets and once again entered private right-of-way with third rail operation. In the distance, the track curves west to start its climb to the C&NW/EJ&E bridge. A. W. JOHNSON / RICHARD ALLERMANN COLLECTION.

140 • Sunset Lines

The most elaborate structure on the Geneva branch was this double set of bridges just west of West Chicago which carried the CA&E up and over both the EJ&E tracks as well as the C&NW branch from West Chicago to Crystal Lake. Late October of 1937 found a CA&E steel 400 series car crossing over the bridge while an EJ&E freight passed underneath. A. W. JOHNSON / RICHARD ALLERMANN COLLECTION.

A short, single-ended siding near High Lake was occasionally used for meets. High Lake was 2.2 miles west of Geneva Junction and trains were normally permitted four to six minutes running time for this distance.

Just west of High Lake, trains changed from third rail to trolley power and shortly thereafter left the private right-of-way and began operating west on the streets of West Chicago. The route continued as a single track down Main Street, which had earlier been called Depot Street since it passed in front of the Chicago & North Western depot.

The interurban trains continued west on Main Street, which made a wide turn to the north adjacent to the C&NW tracks and station. Running time from Wheaton to West Chicago's storefront station was normally 14 minutes. The interurban station was located on the west side of Main Street, just south of Washington, and only a short walk north of the C&NW station.

From a historical standpoint, it is interesting to note that the Geneva branch was the only one of the four CA&E branch lines to the Fox River which passed through a large community between Wheaton and the river. Unfortunately, this distinction had little revenue value for the Geneva branch since the Chicago & North Western provided a faster and more direct service between West Chicago and Chicago.

At the time the interurban was constructed, Main and Fremont Streets did not line up with each other where they intersected Washington. In later years, the city moved the street slightly so that traffic would not have to make a slight jog on Washington to get from Main to Fremont. The single track continued north on Fremont and a brief stop was made at Grand Avenue. Here, the track left city streets for private right-of-way, and train crews hooked down the trolley pole and once more went to third rail power. Records show that the street operation in West Chicago was .88 mile long.

Leaving the Grand Avenue stop, the track made a wide turn to head west once again, and motormen usually built up speed before reaching a large fill. The fill led to a pair of through truss bridges which carried the CA&E up and over both the EJ&E track as well as the C&NW branch from West Chicago to Crystal Lake. Returning to grade, the track soon reached the double-ended West Chicago siding. Located 4.1 miles from Geneva Junction, the siding was occasionally used as a meeting point for trains.

Continuing west from West Chicago siding, the CA&E track passed through a rather unpopulated and occasionally marshy area for the next few miles. A small stop named Kress Road was located adjacent to the crossing of Kress Creek and Kress Road. The next stop was at Kautz Road, which was the dividing line between DuPage and Kane Counties. Then, the stop at Kirk Road was reached where a double-ended siding was used for occasional passenger meets. The distance from West Chicago siding to Kirk siding was 3.4 miles.

Above: The fast portion of the ride was over when the Geneva branch reached the Fox River and turned south on Illinois Highway 25 to head into Geneva. At this point the crew would switch from third rail to trolley wire operation. On October 30, 1937, CA&E Pullman car #412 switches from trolley to third rail as it leaves Highway 25 and heads east to Chicago. The Fox River can be seen between the trees in the background. A. W. JOHNSON / RICHARD ALLERMANN COLLECTION.

Below: The station in Geneva was located on busy State Street. In true interurban fashion, the CA&E cars would load in the center of the street. This 1917 view shows an AE&C car loading on State Street in Geneva while on a run to St. Charles. BARNEY NEUBURGER / RICHARD ALLERMANN COLLECTION.

Most trains were scheduled at 5 minutes between these two points, a reflection of fast running and a lack of important passenger stops.

West of Kirk Road the CA&E track began entering the outskirts of Geneva. At one point a stop was located at Good Templar Park on the eastern end of Geneva, near Dodson Road. From here, the track continued west to Illinois Highway 25 (Riverside Avenue) on the east bank of the Fox River. At this point, the CA&E cars once again put up their trolley poles and followed Highway 25 south along the river. At State Street, the main east-west street of Geneva, the track turned west and both the street and track crossed the Fox River on an interesting concrete arch bridge.

The intersection at 3rd Street was known as Chicago Junction since the Fox River interurban line from Aurora arrived from the south on 3rd Street and turned west on State. This junction was located in the street and was 9.4 miles from Geneva Junction and 37.1 miles from Wells Street Terminal in Chicago. Running time from Wheaton was 25-30 minutes and from Downtown Chicago it was about 1½ hours. Chicago Junction marked the official end of track ownership by the CA&E, as trackage south and west of this point was owned by the Fox River interurban line.

Shortly after service to Geneva began, the AE&C made arrangements with the Fox River interurban line to use two miles of this track to extend service from Geneva to St. Charles. All of the track was located in the street and powered by trolley wire. From Chicago Junction in Geneva, trains would continue west on State Street to Wheelers siding, a distance of $6/10$ of a mile. From here, trains turned north on Anderson Boulevard and Third Street and ran north $9/10$ of a mile to St. Charles siding, located in the street. Trains then completed the last ½ mile by continuing north to Main Street of St. Charles, and then turning east on Main and crossing the Fox River. The St. Charles station and siding were located on Main Street on the east side of the Fox River.

There are three interesting points regarding this extension into St. Charles. First, the Fox River Line operated on the west side of the Fox River between Geneva and St. Charles, but crossed over to the east side on Main Street in St. Charles. Hence, a *westbound* CA&E car arriving from Chicago entered St. Charles going *east*, and an *eastbound* car departing St. Charles for Chicago left heading *west*, certainly a most confusing situation for some passengers. Second, by virtue of the extension to St. Charles, the CA&E at one time provided service to Chicago from all the major communities along the Fox River between Aurora and Elgin. The third interesting point is that the Fox River interurban service between Aurora and Elgin was discontinued in 1935, although the CA&E continued to use the two miles of track between Geneva and St. Charles for two more years. When service to St. Charles ended, it left only the street trackage in Aurora and the freight line at South Elgin (which later became the trolley museum) as the last segments of Aurora Elgin & Fox River trackage still in operation.

The Geneva branch had no known industrial sidings and no railroad interchanges other than with the Fox River electric lines at Geneva. Hence, there was no regular freight train operation over this branch. However, former employees indicate that a conventional railroad tank car was occasionally hauled over the branch as part of a work train to spray the right-of-way. The substantial street operation in West Chicago and Geneva would most likely have precluded any extensive operation of carload freight had such business developed.

Icicles were hanging from the roof of CA&E car #429 on a cold February day in 1935 when it prepared to depart Main Street in St. Charles for Chicago. Although headed east, the car was actually pointing west since it followed the Fox River Trolley tracks across to the west side of the river and south to Geneva. The Baker Hotel and Fox River bridge can be seen in the distance. RICHARD ALLERMANN COLLECTION.

The big "S" curve just east of Halsted Street was a problem for CA&E (and rapid transit) motormen since it required a speed reduction. However, for the photographer it was a marvelous location to find trains on an elevated curve with Chicago's loop for a background. During the evening rush hour of June 19, 1953, a westbound CA&E train (left) passes an eastbound on the curve. ROBERT A. SELLE / RICHARD ALLERMANN COLLECTION.

13

Photographs

The Collingbourne stop on the Elgin branch was situated between the Milwaukee Road and Chicago & North Western underpasses, virtually across the river from the State Mental Hospital. Collingbourne's lack of passengers was somewhat compensated for by its popularity with the photographers as shown by this view of Cincinntati car #421 passing the stop. W. C. JANSSEN.

The Kedzie Avenue station was a regular stop for CA&E trains. A four-car train of St. Louis cars headed by #55 makes a stop here in August of 1946. The St. Louis cars were still relatively new at this date. W. C. JANSSEN / RICHARD ALLERMANN COLLECTION.

A power house and shops for the "L" were located near Racine Street in the center of the elevated structure. This necessitated a slight deviation in trackage as each pair of elevated tracks went around the buildings. Pullman car #413 heads a rush hour train towards the end of elevated operation after adjacent buildings were taken down. TRUMAN HEFNER / GREG HEIER COLLECTION.

Cincinnati car #427 heads a four-car rush hour train west from Des Plaines Avenue. Note the rapid transit train in the rear turning on the CTA loop track which crossed over the CA&E tracks. The expressway was eventually located on a few feet south (right) of where car #427 is in this photo. W. C. JANSSEN.

LEFT: Operation over the Chicago elevated tracks was one of the most unique features of the Chicago Aurora & Elgin. In August of 1953, Pullman car #414 leads a long rush-hour train through the Kedzie station. Operation over the "L" by the CA&E would cease only one month later. TRUMAN HEFNER / LARRY KOSTKA COLLECTION.

RIGHT: St. Louis car #453 heads west out of Chicago on a cold winter day in the early 1950's. The location is the famous Halsted Street curve on Chicago's near west side. In the background is Chicago's Loop and adjacent buildings. TRUMAN HEFNER / GREG HEIER COLLECTION.

Several Chicago Aurora & Elgin passenger cars survived beyond abandonment and continue to operate at various railroad museums. Cincinnati car #431 is shown in 1982 carrying visitors at the Illinois Railway Museum at Union, Illinois. Car #431 was used as the model for the cover illustration on this book. LARRY PLACHNO.

Locomotives #3003-3004 are switching on the McGraw Electric siding near Renwick on the Elgin branch. BARNEY NEUBURGER / RICHARD ALLERMANN COLLECTION.

The date was February 16, 1946, when St. Louis cars #455-452-456 crossed Liberty Drive just east of the Wheaton yard. The new St. Louis cars had only been in service a few weeks when this photo was taken. GORDON E. LLOYD / LARRY PLACHNO COLLECTION.

The new terminal in Aurora opened in 1939. It pleased passengers because of its modern high-level platforms and pleased the photographers because of its proximity to the Fox River. Three cars was a rather substantial train for the Aurora branch and taxed the terminal platform almost to capacity. TRUMAN HEFNER / GREG HEIER COLLECTION.

RIGHT: In 1951, two cars have just arrived in Wheaton off the branches. The conductor of Pullman car #403 prepares to take on passengers while the two cars are coupled for the continuing trip east to Chicago. ROBERT W. GIBSON / LARRY KOSTKA COLLECTION.

OPPOSITE PAGE: Located between Lombard and Glen Ellyn, the Glen Oak stop took its name from the nearby Glen Oak County Club. In addition to being the center of a long high-speed stretch of double track without grade crossings, Glen Oak was also a favorite location for the photographers. WILLIAM E. ROBERTSON.

CA&E Cincinnati car #425 is running as a single car northwest of Wayne and not far from the West Wayne siding and scale track. The adjacent farm land makes a very different background than the suburbs east of Wheaton. TRUMAN HEFNER / GREG HEIER COLLECTION.

Portions of the Batavia branch could be easily compared with less substantial but more typical Midwestern interurban lines. On a warm, post-war Sunday afternoon the Batavia shuttle car completes another run. The date was August 24, 1947, and Pullman car #418 was operating under trolley wire near the Batavia station. VICTOR G. WAGNER.

The CA&E provided carload freight service over most of its tracks. Here, locomotives #4006-4005 are switching at the CB&Q interchange on the north side of Aurora. These were the two largest freight locomotives ever operated by the CA&E. W. C. JANSSEN.

RIGHT: August of 1952 found this four-car train at the Elgin terminal. The various colors of the cars are reflected in the Fox River. TRUMAN HEFNER / LARRY KOSTKA COLLECTION.

PREVIOUS PAGE: The Chicago Aurora & Elgin also operated in the dead of winter when most photographers stayed indoors. This St. Louis car was operating under trolley wire adjacent to the Fox River while coming into Batavia. TRUMAN HEFNER / GREG HEIER COLLECTION.

Index

Page numbers shown in *italics* indicate primary subject or location of photographs.

— A —
Ardmore 60, *61*
Aurora *90*, 91, *104*, 105, *105*, *106*, *107*, *153*, *157*
Aurora Avenue *90*, 101, *103*, *157*
Aurora Substation 101, *102*
Aurora Terminal Siding 105, *107*
Austin Avenue 41
— B —
Baltimore & Ohio Chicago Terminal RR 41
Batavia 109, 115, *116*, 117, *117*, *155*, *156*
Batavia Junction *101*, 101, 109, *110*
Batavia Power House 109, *114*, *115*, 115
Bellwood 51, *55*, *56*, 71, *72*, *77*
Berkeley *57*
Bilter Road 109, *112*
Broadway, Aurora 105, *107*
Butterfield Road 109, *112*
Bypass Route 23, 73, 97
— C —
California Avenue, Chicago 37, *38*
Canal Street, Chicago 37
Canterbury Street 77, *79*
Cermak Road 77, *79*
Chicago & North Western RR 65, 66, 67, 68, 69, 81, 118, 119, 121, 127, 129, 131, 139, 140, 141, 145
Chicago Avenue, Wheaton 91
Chicago Burlington & Quincy RR 90, 101, 103, 107, 111, 114, 115, 157
Chicago Golf 91, *95*
Chicago Great Western RR 41, *43*, 47, 51, *55*, *56*, *58*, *61*, 119
Chicago Junction 143
Chicago Lake Shore & South Bend RR 20
Chicago Loop 27
Chicago Milwaukee St. Paul & Pacific RR 130, 131, 133, 145
Chicago North Shore & Milwaukee RR 22, 25, 73
Chicago Rapid Transit Co. 54, 77, *78*, *79*
Chicago South Shore & South Bend RR 20, *24*
Chicago Surface Lines 30
Chicago Transit Authority 77, *148*
Chicago Wheaton & Western RR 137
Chicago Westchester & Western RR 73, 77
Childs Street, Wheaton *94*
Church Road 101, *102*

Cicero Avenue, Chicago 37
Clintonville *129*, 131
Coleman 127, *143*
College Avenue 68, *69*
Collingbourne *130*, 131, *131*, *145*
Dr. Thomas Conway 19, *23*
— D —
Des Plaines Avenue (see Forest Park)
Des Plaines River Bridge 51, *54*
Diehl Road 97, *100*
— E —
East Warrenville (see Mont View)
Eggert Siding 135
Electroliners *18*
Elgin *132*, *133*, *134*, 135, *135*, *157*
Elgin & Belvidere Electric *133*, 135
Elgin Joliet & Eastern RR ... 100, 101, 127, 128, 141
Elgin Joliet & Eastern Interchanges *100*, 101, 127, *128*
Elgin Junction 127, *128*
Elmhurst 57, *58*, *59*
Emory 91, *94*
Eola Junction 109
Eola Road 109
Everett-Moore Syndicate 19
— F —
Fanette 137
Ferry Road 97
Fessler Road 125
Fifth Avenue, Maywood 51, *54*
Forest Park 44, *45*, *46*, *47*, *48*, *49*, *148*
Fox River Trolley Museum *160*
— G —
Garden Home 57
Gary Siding 97
Geneva *142*, 143
Geneva Junction 119, 137, *139*
Geneva Road 119
Glen Ellyn 65, *67*, *69*
Glen Oak 65, *65*, *66*, *152*
Glenwood Park 109, 111, *114*, *115*, 115
Good Templar Park 143
Grand Avenue, West Chicago *140*, 141
Green Valley *64*, 65
Gunderson Avenue 41, *42*
— H —
Halsted St. 32, 37, *144*, *149*
Harlem Avenue 41, *43*
Harrison Street 71, *70*, *74*, 77

158 • Sunset Lines

Hart Road	109, *113*
High Lake	137, *139*
Hollywood	*130*, 131
Hoyne, Chicago	37

— I —

Illinois Avenue, Aurora	*104*, 105
Illinois Central RR	57, 58, 71, 73, 75, 77, 127, *128*
Illinois Railway Museum	*149*
Illinois Terminal RR	21
Indiana Harbor Belt RR	51, 57, 71, 73
Samuel Insull	19, 21, 27, 33

— J —

Jefferson Electric Co.	51
Jernstrom's Gardens	71
Jewell Road	119
Joliet Road Siding	97

— K —

Kautz Road	141
Kedzie Avenue, Chicago	37, *146*, 148
Kilbourn Avenue, Chicago	37, *39*
Kirk Road	141
Kress Road	*136*, 141

— L —

Lakewood	123, *124*, 125
Laramie Avenue	37, *40*
Lavergne Avenue, Chicago	37, *39*
Liberty Street, Wheaton	81, *85*, 119, 121, *151*
Lincoln Avenue	119, *122*
"Little Joe"	20, 23
Lockwood Yard	23, 37, *41*
Lombard	61, *62*, 63, 65

— M —

Madison Street	74
Main Street, Glen Ellyn	67, 69
Main Street, Lombard	63, 65
Mannheim Road	56, 71, 73, 76, 79
Marshfield Junction	36, 37
Maywood	51, *54*, 55
McCormick Siding	91
McGraw/Toastmaster Siding	*130*, 131
Metropolitan West Side Elevated	27, 33, 111
Michigan City	24
Milwaukee Road (see Chicago Milwaukee St. Paul & Pacific RR)	
Mont View	97, *98*
Mont View Siding	97
Mt. Carmel Cemetery	71, 73

— N —

National Street, Elgin	131, *132*, 133
New York Street, Aurora	*105*, 105
North Shore Line (See Chicago North Shore & Milwaukee RR)	

— O —

Oak Park Avenue	42
Oak Ridge Cemetery	71, 73
Ogden Avenue, Chicago	37

— P —

Pacific Electric	24
Pennsylvania RR	37
Plamondon	91, *95*, 96
Pleasant Hill	119
Pomeroy-Mandelbaum Syndicate	19
Poplar Avenue	57
Prince Crossing	119, *123*
Pulaski Road, Chicago	37

— Q —

— R —

Racine Street, Chicago	36, 37, 37, *147*
Radant Road	109, 115
Renwick	*130*, 131, *150*
Roosevelt Road, Westchester	71, 77, *78*
Roosevelt Road, Wheaton	91

— S —

Sacramento Avenue, Chicago	37, *38*
St. Andrews	125
St. Charles	143, *143*
St. Charles Road	*127*, 127
St. Louis Avenue, Chicago	37
Seventeenth Avenue, Maywood	51, *55*
Skokie Valley Line	19, 23
Smith Road	*125*, 125
Soo Line RR	41, *43*
South Elgin Sand & Gravel Co.	*129*, 131
South Shore Line (see Chicago South Shore & South Bend RR)	
Spring Road	57, *59*
Standard Oil Siding	89
State Road	109, *112*
Stewart Avenue	*62*, 65
Stratford Hills	57

— T —

Taylor Avenue	65, *66*
Twenty-Fifth Avenue, Bellwood	*50*, 51
Twenty-Second Street, Westchester (see Cermak Road)	

— U —

Union Station, Chicago	37

— V —

Villa Avenue	*59*, 60, 61
Villa Park	*59*, 60, 61
Vulcan Stamping & Mfg. Co.	75

— W —

Wagner Road	109, *113*
Warrenville	97, *99*
Warrenville Siding	97
Wayne	126, 127, *154*
Wayne Scale Track	*126*, 127
Weisbrook Road	91, 97
Wells Street Terminal	26, 27, 28, 29, 30, 31
Wesley Street	119
West Chicago	139, 140, 141, *141*
West Towns Railway	37, 41, 47
Westchester	73, 77, *77*, 78, 79
Western Avenue, Chicago	37
Westmore	61, *62*
Wheaton	69, *80*, 81, *83*, 83, 84, 85, 86, 88, 89, 119, 121, *153*
Wheaton Shop	83, *86*, 87
Williams Road	97
Winfield Road	97, *98*, 137
Wolf Road	57, *58*, 71

— X —

— Y —

York Road	57

— Z —

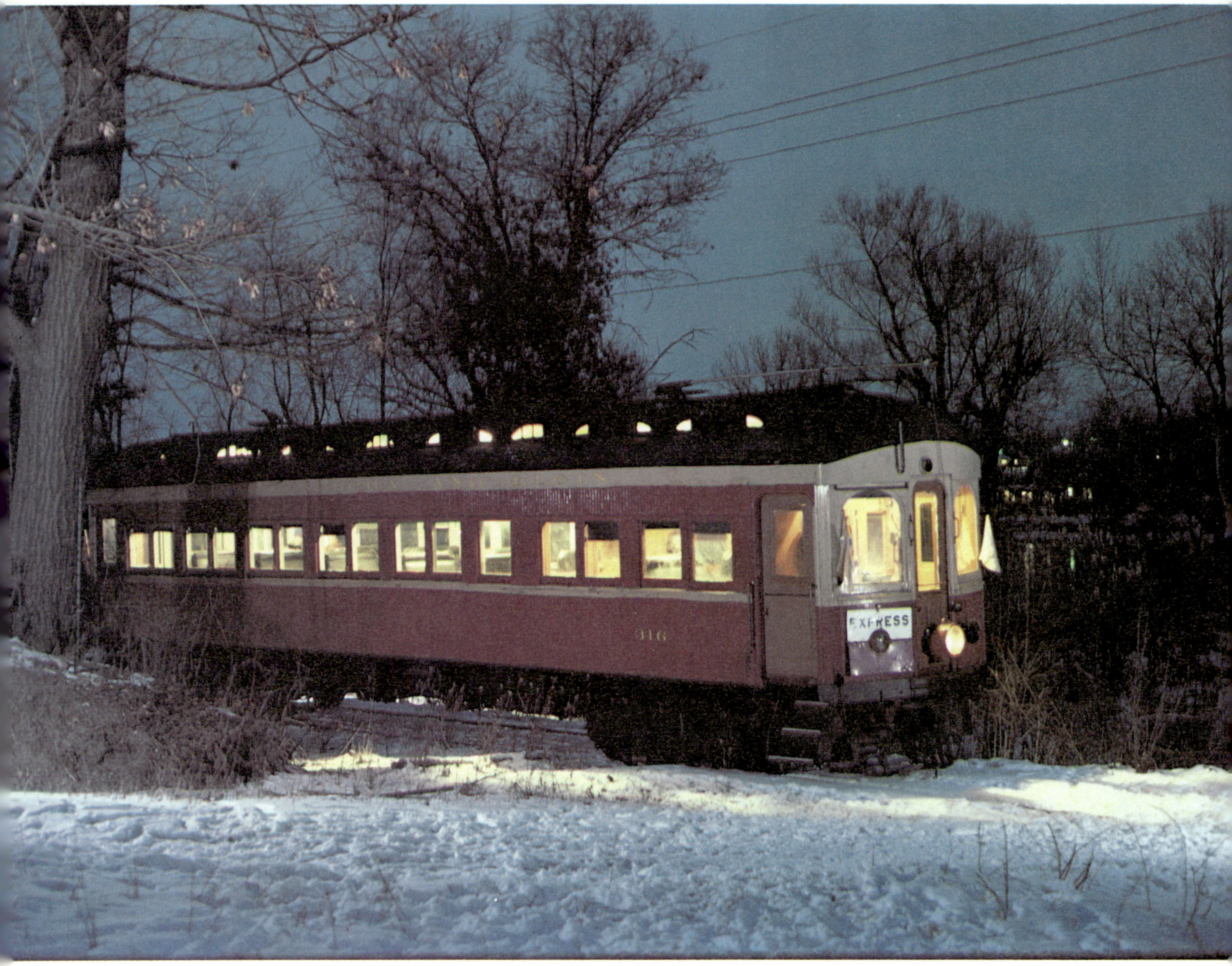

Although the Chicago Aurora & Elgin ceased operations over a quarter of a century ago, some of its cars continue to operate in various railroad and trolley museums. Those interested have an opportunity to ride on one of these cars to get some idea of what it was like to ride on "Sunset Lines." In February of 1975, CA&E car #316 was making a night run at the Fox River Trolley Museum in South Elgin, Illinois. LARRY KOSTKA.

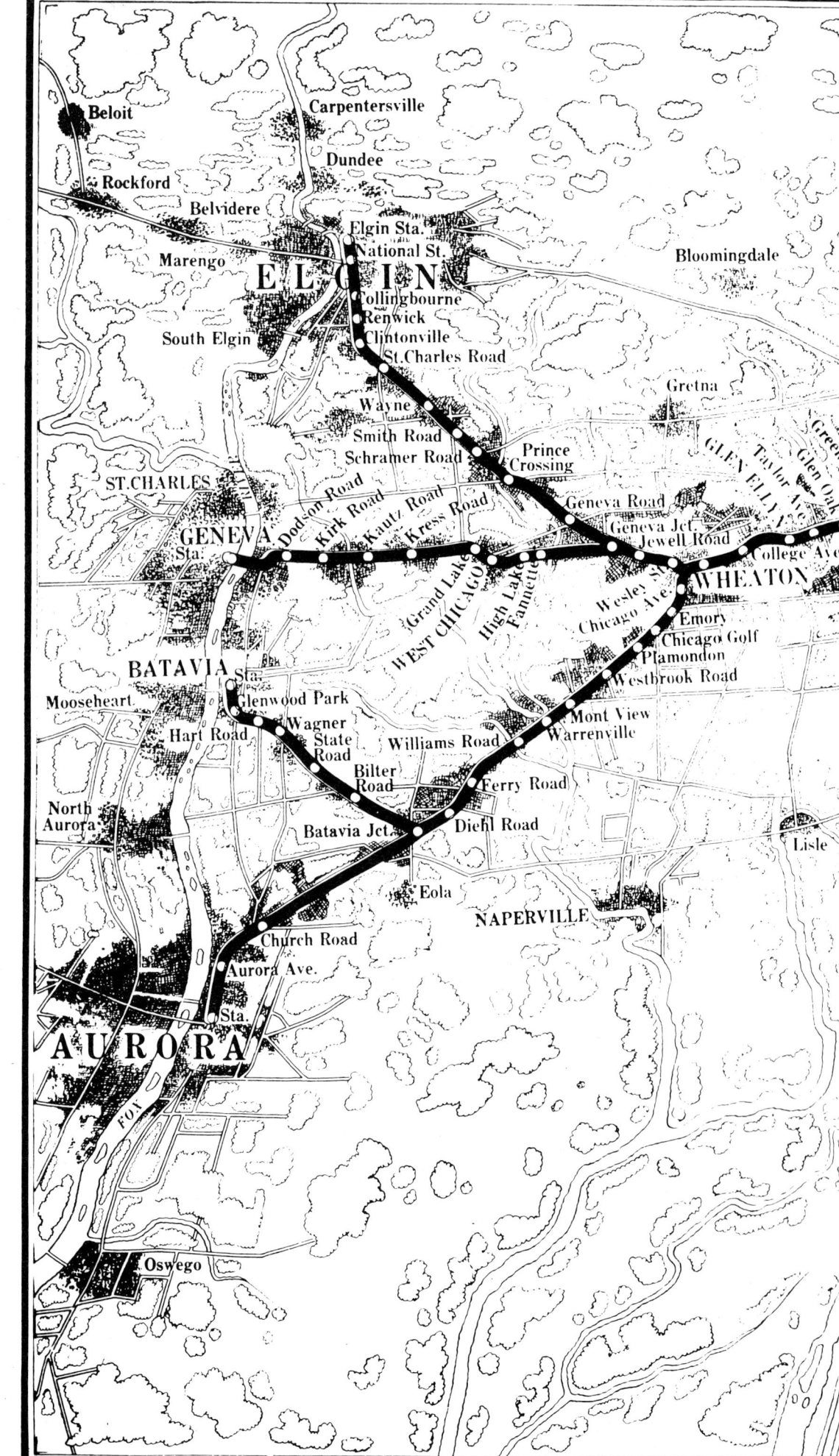